C000111409

The School of Fashion: A Novel

SCHOOL OF FASHION,

A NOVEL.

IN THREE VOLUMES.

VOL. II.

LONDON:

HENRY COLBURN, NEW BURLINGTON STREET.

1829.

LONDON:

Printed by J. L. Cox, Great Queen Street
Lincoln's-Inn Fields

823
Sch65
v. 2

THE

SCHOOL OF FASHION.

CHAPTER I.

MRS. LOVAINE meditated much as to the manner in which it was best to conduct herself under the difficult circumstances in which we have just quitted her; and the result was a determination to increase her own attentions to and intimacy with Lord Goldsborough; and in no way to interfere for the present with the pursuits of Mr. William De Clifford; hoping by these means ultimately to secure to her daughter the rank and situation, for which, according to her ideas, she was so eminently fitted; and in the interval to avoid the risk of her being, even for a short time, without admirers. She deemed it expedient, upon the whole, not openly to allude to her views upon the subject to Elinor; although she anticipated no difficulty as likely to arise on her part in throwing off Mr. De Clifford when necessary, and was troubled with no scruples of conscience at the idea of his being so thrown off.

" He is only," thought she to herself, " a poor younger brother, who never can think of marrying, and who has therefore no business to fall in love himself; and still less to try and engage my dear child's affections. Happily I have such perfect confidence in Elinor's discretion and good conduct, that I am quite at ease on that score; but I could not possibly pity him for a disappointment of his own creation, which he in fact deserves."

Thus reasoned Mrs. Lovaine! and thus has reasoned many a mother before her, when, blinded by maternal vanity and worldly ambition, they forget, (in their anxiety, that, at all risks, due homage should be paid to their daughter's charms) that younger brothers have as much power to feel pain or pleasure, as the heir-apparent, if not more; that they will consider themselves encouraged when they are so; and that a young lady, though very well conducted, and extremely amiable, may look forward with reasonable hopes of happiness to an union with the object of her choice, although that object be rather possessed of competency than of riches, and that he could not afford to *do nothing;* and in short, though he should have the misfortune of being one of that tribe, so correctly and judiciously termed by a lady of fashion, " Detrimentals."

Fresh appointments were made by Mrs. Lovaine, for the cultivation of Lord Goldsborough's taste for music, or for Elinor; and with far better success than that which attended her first attempt. Elinor also soon became more reconciled to these morning practices, being seldom called upon for her share in the performance; for as Mrs. Lovaine generally found him most disposed to fix a future hour to repeat the agreeable visit, when he had been

the principal or sole performer, she had the
wisdom no longer to insist on the superior
merits of a duet; indeed, though she considered it her duty to give Elinor every possible
opportunity of establishing herself to advantage, she seldom failed mentioning to those
with whom she discussed such interesting
topics, her determination never to interfere in
her daughter's choice; as well as her conviction of the folly, if not wickedness, of trying
to force the inclinations of young people.

Lord Goldsborough would sometimes bring
his guitar, (on which, to the ears of those who
were impartial to him, and partial to music,
he played remarkably ill,) and as he did not
discover that Mrs. Lovaine always nodded her
head out of time, and smiled most compla-

cently when he sang the most out of tune, he
was much gratified at the unequivocal admiration which she evinced, and at the unqualified
praise which she bestowed at the close of every
little easy national air to which he had accompanied himself on his instrument. He was
indeed the more gratified, as his birth-right had
procured him no such advantages from Lady
Harriet and Miss De Clifford; or indeed from
most of the society then assembled at Spa. Not
that all were indifferent to his good graces,
but that, from a variety of causes too trifling
to be recorded, his imaginary talent had been
insufficiently appreciated; and he was on that
account the more susceptible to the flattery
of Mrs. Lovaine.

Had Elinor appeared equally delighted with

all he said or did, he would probably, as on many former occasions, have taken instant alarm; but he often met Mr. De Clifford and his sister there, and could not fail to perceive that the former was fully as well, and the latter openly much better received by Miss Lovaine than himself. She was civil enough never to mortify his *amour propre*, and yet not so civil as to arouse his wonted prudence, by awakening the rememberance of the possibility of being entrapped. They seldom conversed much together. He silently approved of her docility and ready obedience to her mother's wishes, but it was to the latter that he attached himself principally in private, and wholly in public; nor was he at all displeased at being occasionally rallied by a young acquaintance (who was

always anxious to make himself agreeable to
those who might have it in their power to be
useful to him in return) upon his attentions to
Mrs. Lovaine, for though he shrunk with horror
from the idea of being caught by any girl, and
would repel with virtuous indignation the base
accusation of courting the affections of an *un-
married* .lady, his vanity was so flattered at
being thought the favoured suitor of one who
had solemnly vowed eternal fidelity to another,
that he could never bring himself upon such
occasions to give more than a chuckling denial,
which at once satisfied his own conscience, and
confirmed the flattering suspicion.

· With this state of affairs Lord Goldsborough
was gratified, Mrs. Lovaine sanguine, Elinor
quiescent, William De Clifford hopeful, and

all apparently bid fair to all, for the fulfilment
of wishes, however absolutely opposed to and
incompatible with each other.

" How melancholy poor Mr. Gordon looks!"
remarked Elinor one day to William de Clifford, " can he have any cause of unhappiness,
or is it his nature to be low spirited ?"

" I fear, poor fellow! that Emily must
charge her conscience with much of his present
want of enjoyment. I know not whether she
will ever make him honourable amends for his
pains, but I am sure he deserves her, if perseverance and attachment can entitle him to that
reward."

" I have sometimes observed that he looked
annoyed, when he saw your sister talking and
dancing so merrily with others, but I was not

aware of the extent to which he did her justice, or that his happiness so much depended upon her—it is perhaps," added she with some embarrassment, " rather an impertinent question, but you know how much Emily's fate interests me, and that must plead my excuse: do you wish Mr. Gordon success?"

" Surely, dear Miss Lovaine, you need scarcely apologize for asking me any thing, but still less should you accuse yourself of indiscretion, when you are but giving a proof of that which gives me such sincere pleasure.—I mean your interest and affection for my sister; believe me she is worthy of the love of all who know her. There is not one of us, not even a servant in the house, who would not go to the utmost part of the world to serve her; and few people are so adored in their own home without reason. But" said he, smiling as he checked the warmth with which he was speaking, " I am accused of being rhapsodical on that subject; and moreover I have not yet answered your question. My personal acquaintance with Gordon is small, and though I have the greatest desire to know him better, for the purpose of forming some more distinct wish for or against his success, I am now unfortunately precluded, by our relative situations, from the power of so doing; any advances on the part of her family might mislead with respect to our, or rather to her, feelings towards him. Her happiness is our first object, and till we know whether that would be secured or endangered by such an union, we have no right to persuade or dissuade her, to encourage or discourage him."

" Then you have not yet made up your mind—but as you give me leave to question you, I must ask you whether you think that Emily likes Mr. Gordon; or whether, if she did not like him very much indeed, she would marry him, if Lady Harriet thought fit? Mamma said the other day that she had so good an opinion of Miss De Clifford, that she had no doubt but that she would be guided always in her choice of a husband solely by her mother's wishes."

" My mother would never exert authority upon that point."

" Oh no! Mamma did not mean that— on the contrary, she always says that parents should never force a marriage upon their children—but that it is their duty to give advice, and it is ours to follow it. She says she is sure that Emily would always be disposed to bestow her affections wherever Lady Harriet advised; now though I am sure she would always do whatever is right, I have sometimes doubted whether it would be possible to like a person in compliance with the wishes of any one."

William was half amused, and extremely charmed with the simplicity of Elinor's doubt, as to the extent of the power of volition or obedience; but as he was now generally kindly received by Mrs. Lovaine, and hoped therefore that her influence (if necessary) might one day be exerted in his favour, he avoided replying to her query, and continued the topic of his sister.

" Mrs. Lovaine is mistaken in Emily if she supposes her to be of so ductile a nature; my mother is anxious for her to marry, (though it would be almost death to part with her) but she fears that if her extreme fastidiousness on that point continues, it will be impossible for her ever to do so. I own it is to me, and indeed to all of us, quite inexplicable that a person so exquisitely sensitive, so full of tenderness on all other occasions, should be so insensible to the addresses and the affection of those who are willing to devote their lives to her, who appear unexceptionable to us, and against whom she has so very little to allege. The fact is that Emily's failing (for you know she must have a failing or she would not be human) is being a little too romantic. I do not mean that she is, or ever was, guilty of a mawkish affected sentimentality, which is so often assumed to hide a want of real feeling, and to attract attention; but she is naturally of an enthusiastic turn of mind, and has fixed her ideas of perfection in man, and consequent hopes of happiness in marriage, beyond what I fear it is probable can ever be realized; her motto is, I believe,

" Point de milieu; l'hymen et ses liens

" Sont les plus grands, ou des maux ou des biens."

" Does Lady Harriet recommend her accepting Mr. Gordon? or do you think that he fulfils Emily's expectations?"

" Neither—my mother never will recommend to her to accept any one; and my sister does not, I suspect, consider him the personification of her *beau idéal*, although she has not, at my mother's request, *decided* against him."

" Does she then think that Emily could like him if she endeavoured so to do?"

" She thinks that Emily should give herself more time than she is disposed to do upon such occasions, ere she throws away, what is, in her opinion, an opportunity of establishing herself respectably, and happily. She wishes her not to consider it necessary that an angel should woo her to make " marriage a sample of celestial bliss," and not at once to reject the thought of any man whose only failing is not being more than human."

The conversation was here interrupted by the entrance of little Harry De Clifford, who had been sent by his sister to remind Elinor that the hour at which they had appointed to ride was already past, and to request that the rendezvous might be at their hotel.

William was naturally her escort for the short distance that intervened between the two houses; but Elinor was thoughtful, and scarcely spoke. In quitting the house, they had opened the door to Lord Goldsborough, who at that moment arrived to pay his respects to Mrs. Lovaine, and inquiring of Elinor whether her mother was at home, was by no means deterred from making his visit by perceiving that she would not be present to share its pleasure.

The sight of Lord Goldsborough brought to
Elinor's mind the frequent encomiums passed
upon his character, manners, and appearance,
by Mrs. Lovaine, and the very little disposition
which she had hitherto felt in her own mind to
second such praises. Concluding, at the same
time, from the conversation which had just
passed with William upon the subject of his
sister's over-fastidiousness, that his opinion of
the facility of controlling and directing the affections, coincided, in a great measure, with
that of her mother, she reproached herself
with the want of will, rather than of power,
to see his lordship's merits; and determined
to make amends for her former injustice, by
trying, in future, the extent to which the

power of volition, upon such occasions, could be carried.

Had William anticipated such an application of his prudent and (towards his sister's suitors) charitable discourse, it is possible that poor Elinor would have been spared the expression of his reflections and regrets upon Emily's readiness to start objections, and see defects, which were unadmitted and unperceived by others; *i. e.* had Mr. William De Clifford foreseen that his observations upon Miss De Clifford were likely to produce in Miss Lovaine an endeavour to consider Lord Goldsborough in a more favourable point of view, they would probably have been much qualified, if not entirely withheld.

It is far more easy to prescribe rules for the

tastes and inclinations of others, than to act
upon them ourselves; not that we are incapable of feeling as great, if not a greater,
degree of interest and affection for those whom
we love best, than for ourselves, but that there
is a difficulty, an impossibility of diving into
those innermost thoughts and feelings which
directly or indirectly influence their conduct
and character; and which can, if known at
all, be known only to themselves. This often
renders their motives subject to misappre-
hension or misconstruction; and their actions
liable to creating a surprise and wonder, if not
censure, that would be far from existing, could
they be fathomed or understood.

How often would " I never was so astonished
in my life as at ———'s conduct!" " I could

not have conceived it possible that ———
would have so acted!" " Nothing is to me so
surprising as ———'s taste!" and such like
exclamations be spared, if every one as tho-
roughly understood his neighbour's feelings,
dispositions, principles, and circumstances, as
he affects to do; for how often would he be
obliged to acknowledge that, similarly situated,
he would have thought or acted in like manner.

Perhaps, if William had, by some magic
power, been enabled to read exactly his sister's
character, thoughts, and sentiments, he would
have been speedily convinced that the resem-
blance between himself and her was far too
close to give the right to wonder, and still less
to censure.

CHAPTER II.

THE day following that on which the conversation took place between Elinor and
William, relative to Miss De Clifford's matrimonial, or rather unmatrimonial dispositions,
and which has been duly recorded in the preceding chapter, Lady Harriet was surprised by
the arrival of a visitor at an unusually early
hour. The door opened, and Mr. Gordon was
announced. The gravity of his countenance,
the hour of the morning, and the embarrassment of his manner, soon suggested to Lady
Harriet's mind the purport of his visit; and

when, after expressing a reasonable degree of
fear that he was interrupting her ladyship by
the earliness of his visit, and making a few
very commonplace observations on the weather,
he paused, and a dead silence ensued, poor
Lady Harriet's heart sunk within her. She felt
for his embarrassment, which it was impossible
for her to relieve, by speaking first on the
subject which she was confident it was his
purpose now to broach. She thought it better
for all parties that some communication, respecting his attachment to Emily, should take
place; that the affair should come to some
point, instead of hanging on in the manner it
had done of late, by which he rather increased
his stock of mortification than his chance of
success; and yet she scarcely knew to what

point she wished it to come, or what degree of hope she might be justified in giving him.

Mr. Gordon looked attentively at every seal upon a watch-chain that chanced to be on the table; and turned the wheel of a trinket wheelbarrow, appertaining to the *Charivari*, with a rapidity never destined to belong to its motions, and which effectually prevented its ever performing any future evolution; till at last, thinking that if it were done " 'twere well it were done quickly," he courageously broke the silence, by saying, " I have already apologized for my intrusion—but, perhaps, I ought equally to do so for its purport.

" You have not, perhaps, been as unobservant of, as I sometimes fear your daughter is indifferent to the sentiments with which she has for some time inspired me. You cannot, I am sure, be a stranger to my feelings. May I hope, Lady Harriet, that your influence, the power of which I know to be so great, will be exercised in my favour; or do I flatter myself too much, in believing that you would rather befriend than oppose the fulfilment of my wishes."

"You do but justice to my anxiety as a mother," replied Lady Harriet, "in supposing that your preference for my dear child has not passed unnoticed by me; and I cannot but rejoice at your openness on a subject so very near to my heart as her prospects in life."

Mr. Gordon began to look confident.

"Particularly," continued Lady Harriet, "as by giving me the opportunity of making a candid exposition of my own feelings in this matter, I shall hope to avoid in future all appearance of inconsistency towards you."

Mr. Gordon coloured;—he suspected that what he had just heard was to be a preamble to a painful and mortifying communication.

"Emily," said she, "must be the arbitress of her own fate. She has our permission to please herself. So long as there exists the means of subsistence, we should never offer any opposition on the score of rank or fortune; and there is little doubt of our being perfectly satisfied in other respects, with even less than would probably meet her own wishes. Thus indisposed to offer any opposition to her choice, should she be inclined to make one, still less, as you may imagine, should we ever dream of forcing one upon her. I may try to convince her reason, but would, on no account, wish by any other means to control her actions upon such a subject."

" You mean, then, I fear, to inform me that without the use of undue influence on the part of yourself and Mr. De Clifford, my addresses to Miss De Clifford are not likely to meet with a favourable reception," said Mr. Gordon, whose pride for a moment struggled with the humility with which his passion had inspired him.

" Pardon me," replied Lady Harriet, " you express yourself too strongly; but I have said that I would be perfectly open with you. You shall therefore hear exactly my view of the

case, and you can then judge best for yourself
how to act."

I would be tedious to relate in full the particulars of an interview, fraught with deep
interest to the parties concerned, but of which
the result alone is material to impart. Lady
Harriet declared it to be her opinion, that an
avowal of his feelings and wishes to her daughter, at that moment, would meet with an unfavourable reception, and therefore advised
him against such a step. She professed herself
to be friendly to his suit, as, according to her
conviction, its success was calculated to pro-
mote that which was so near and dear to her
heart, the happiness of her child. "If," said
she, " you are disposed, by following my ad-

vice, to profit by the knowledge which some years' experience has given me of Emily's disposition and character, I will give it you to the best of my power. Remember, however, that as I can neither guarantee its wisdom, or its infallibility, you must not hold me answerable for its failure."

It was then agreed that Miss De Clifford should not be made acquainted with the purport of Mr. Gordon's interview with Lady Harriet that morning; and that, as it would be difficult for him to be less assiduous in his attentions to her, thrown together so repeatedly, as from the habits of the place and the society they unavoidably were, he should quit Spa in the course of a few days, and join them, or not, elsewhere, according as he felt inclined to abandon or continue his present pursuit; for doubtful, as Lady Harriet expressed herself, of what might be the final result of perseverance on the part of Mr. Gordon, she was anxious to impress on his mind, that she did not consider him as committed to any line of conduct, but that which was most congenial to his feelings, or probably conducive to his future happiness, by the avowal which he had just made of his present hopes and wishes. She utterly disclaimed all intention of forwarding his interests by persuasion, or any other means that might influence her daughter's decision in his favour, beyond that of affording such opportunity as he might desire of cultivating her society, and rendering himself agreeable to her.

Mr. Gordon received her communication

with thanks and gratitude. The candour and sincerity which she had displayed inspired him with confidence in her advice; in proof of which, having announced, the first opportunity he had of doing so, in the presence of Emily, his intention of setting out on a tour at the end of the week, he took leave of her when the day arrived, without the slightest allusion to the sentiments with which she had inspired him.

His departure was no small relief to Emily; the dreaded moment when a decision on her part would be called for, was delayed at least, if not altogether avoided. She even flattered herself that, as his manner had been somewhat less demonstrative for a few days previous to that on which he took his leave, and he had sought no explanation, he had either

changed his mind, or that she had been misled
by her mother's over readiness to believe in her
powers of attraction, in thinking such an explanation probable.   Lady Harriet, moreover,
ceased to reason with her upon the subject, a
measure which, in confirmation of her own
opinion, had been enjoined by Mr. De Clifford, to whom the particulars of the interview
we have already described were duly and
fully related by Lady Harriet.

" You have now," said he, as she concluded
her narration, " very properly promised Mr.
Gordon facilities to advance his own cause—you
have told him how best to woo her—and if he
does not succeed, we may fairly suppose that our
dear girl's disinclination to the marriage is too
well-founded, or, at any rate, too great to ren-

der such a step desirable; we must, therefore, be careful to abstain from any further expression of our opinion on the subject, lest, through an imaginary compliance with our wishes, she should sacrifice her own happiness."

No two circumstances could be more favourable to the success of Mr. Gordon's suit than this silence on the part of her family, and his own absence; not that Mr. De Clifford was mistaken in the supposition that she might be influenced by their wishes, but because she imagined that their silence proceeded from a tacit acknowledgment of their having given an undue degree of importance to his attentions; and that they, like herself, no longer anticipated the dreaded call for decision. She, in short, ceased to consider him as an unfavoured suitor, and only thought of him as one to whom she had often acted (under a mistaken impression) with a want of courtesy, almost amounting to a want of civility, and for which she felt in duty bound to atone, should they ever meet again.

It has been remarked by Voltaire " *qu'on se rend insupportable dans la société par des défauts légers, qui se font sentir à tous momens,*" and never was there a more just observation. It is indeed often more difficult to bear with the weaknesses and foibles, than with the graver faults and vices of our neighbours; that is, so long as we are exposed to the inconveniences of the former. By absence, we cease to be reminded each moment of their existence; however when reason and reflection take place

of irritation and prejudice, and we allow ourselves to make a cool and impartial comparison
between the magnitude of the offences, and the
degree of blame they ought justly to incur, the
heavier sins rise up in judgment against us,
whilst the lighter are almost forgotten; we reproach ourselves for the moral injustice of
misplaced severity; and sometimes, in a fit of
repentance, exalt every negative quality into a
positive virtue. Thus the dull man, who has
not the wit to discover the little ridicules and
absurdities of others, is dignified with the title
of good-natured—the man who does not cheat,
with that of honourable—the man alike indifferent to the charms of woman and of the
gaming-table, is reckoned high-principled—he
who never speaks, is commended as one who

slanders not his neighbour—and those who are incapable of ever forming an opinion of their own, are always said to be candid and unprejudiced.

Now, although Mr. Gordon had some very real and substantial merits, he certainly was one of those characters that gained in estimation rather by absence than by intercourse; and ere he had very long quitted her whom he sought to please, she was far more disposed to consider him worthy of being liked and esteemed, than when she had daily, if not hourly, opportunities of improving her acquaintance with him.

CHAPTER III.

ABOUT a fortnight from the time at which our last chapter closed, was that which was fixed for the departure of the De Clifford family from Spa.

> " Tis hard to be parted from those
> With whom we for ever could dwell."

So thought the junior members of the party, whilst assembled together for the last time at Lady Harriet's hotel. There is always something particularly melancholy in doing a thing for the last time: even that which may have imparted more of pain than of pleasure, often

changes its character in our eyes when we
believe it never likely to be beheld again.
But in the present instance all had been pleasure; the party who now met under that roof
for the last time, had never met there but to
please and to be pleased. At times they talked
and laughed as much and as heartily as ever,
but these little bursts were occasionally succeeded by those dead silences which soon betray that " the spirits flag below."

The hour was late before the Lovaines rose
to take leave. The Count Povolowski offered
his arm to Mrs. Lovaine, whilst William De
Clifford tendered his to conduct Elinor home.

It was a night well calculated to excite those
feelings of awe and melancholy which the consideration of time and eternity, and the in-

stability of all earthly affairs, can never fail to inspire. " In the sky the stars were met,"— the moon was bright; not a breath of wind was to be felt, and every sound was hushed. " All was so still, so soft in earth and air," that, as if afraid of disturbing the serenity of all around, both William and Elinor remained for some time silent.

" How impossible is it," said William at last, as they drew near the end of their walk, " to part from those with whom one has been living some time in the daily interchange of thoughts and words, and that have afforded unrivalled pleasure, without reflecting on the utter uncertainty of all human events. The possibility that some of us may never meet again in this world, and the almost certainty,

should we all meet again, that time, and
change of place and circumstances, must, and
will, have produced a certain degree of change
in feeling towards each other."

The tears started into Elinor's eyes; she had
never before felt so sad, and yet she scarcely
knew why; for, as we mentioned elsewhere,
she had not yet learned to analyse her own
feelings and motives. That she was sad, however, was sufficient to produce as satisfactory
an appearance of sorrow and regret in her
manner, when she bade adieu to William, as
even he could require.

The parting between Mrs. Lovaine and her
cavalier was less pathetic. Count Povolowski
had given Elinor credit rather for obedience
than caprice in her conduct towards him; and

though he was undoubtedly a little disappointed
that she had not been too fully impressed with
his charms to be so dutiful a daughter, yet he
comforted his vanity by the belief that nothing
short of the fear of her mother could have produced such insensibility; he was therefore
still in charity with her.

With Mrs. Lovaine however, as may be
supposed, he was not over pleased, and neither
was he wholly unrevenged. Much as she at
first dreaded his interference with the higher
objects she had in view for Elinor, she had not
observed his increased intimacy with the De
Cliffords, or heard it remarked that the Count
was one of Miss De Clifford's many willing
victims, with absolute indifference. She would
rather have heard him pitied as the dejected

and rejected suitor of her own daughter, than mentioned as the gay admirer of another. He shrewdly suspected this, and determined to afford her no such gratification. Moreover, as he resolved to quit Spa on the same day as those to whom he had transferred his attentions, he could not resist the satisfaction of endeavouring, in this his last interview, in some degree to shame her for the caprice which she had evinced towards him.

He praised Emily generally, but so particularly for those qualities in which Mrs. Lovaine knew she differed most from Elinor, that her maternal pride was far from gratified; but when he drew, what her conscience told her was a comparison between Lady Harriet and herself, her vanity was greatly mortified, and she inwardly determined never again to be too *prévenante*, on first acquaintance, to foreigners, or to others who were ineligible as husbands for her girl, lest she should undergo similar farewell conversations, after she had been under the necessity of repelling the intimacy she had courted.

" Lady Harriet," said the Count, " est d'un caractère charmant, charmant; aussi elle a des manières comme il n-y en a pas ! elle a tant de dignité sans hauteur, tant d'esprit sans préten- tion, tant de grâce sans affectation ! Elle n'est jamais journalière. Elle ne vous accueille pas comme Prince un jour pour vous chasser comme Valet le lendemain. Il n-y-a rien qui dégoute comme l'inconséquence et le caprice; rien de si choquant que de ne savoir à quelle réception s'attendre. Elle ne fait jamais sentir à un étranger qu'il est indigne de l'approcher au moment où elle voudroit se vouer à quelque jeune et riche Milor. Il faut avouer qu'elle ne vous flatte pas la vanité jusqu'au point de vous faire la cour, mais de l'autre côté, elle ne blesse jamais l'amour-propre par cette absence de bienveillance, qui fait voir qu'on n'est bien reçu qu'en pis-aller."

Mrs. Lovaine endeavoured to interrupt these unpleasant encomiums upon the beauty and consistency of Lady Harriet's character, by asking him whether he intended to pass the following winter at Rome. He replied in the affirmative, adding, with some emphasis, " Puisqu'on m'y fait meilleur accueil qu'autre part je crois que je ferai bien d'y rester toujours."

With this, and a few more similar observations, Count Povolowski wound up his farewell discourse with Mrs. Lovaine; who, vexed and mortified at its tenor, was far from regretting the moment when, by their arrival at her house, she was relieved from his presence.

By the time that Elinor and her mother met at breakfast the following morning, a few only of those with whom they had been living in habits of friendship and intimacy remained at Spa; and both experienced much of that gloomy re-action which generally succeeds a previous state of joyous excitement. Mrs. Lovaine was much disappointed that Elinor had had no offers to reject from either of the individuals whom she did not intend her to accept, and still more at her having none from him whom she so ardently wished to be, but whom she almost despaired now of ever seeing, her son-in-law. She would even have reproached herself with having managed her daughter's concerns very badly, had she not remembered in time for her own peace of mind, that having fulfilled to the utmost of her power the duty she owed to her child, she was not answerable for the failure of designs thus suggested by natural affection and anxiety.

Elinor's whole countenance bore unequivocal signs of a sleepless night; she complained of head-ache, and, retiring to her room immediately after breakfast, little or nothing passed between her and her mother relative to the past pleasure or prospective dulness of their *séjour* at Spa.

It was fated, however, that the day should not close without affording Mrs. Lovaine the most soothing consolation in moments like the present—the birth of new hopes. Her future movements depended upon letters from home, which could not reach her for at least a week or ten days. Lord Goldsborough's plans also depended upon letters from England; but as his were expected to arrive by that day's post, and his departure was in consequence fixed for the following morning, Mrs. Lovaine concluded, when she saw him approach the house, that he was come to make his *adieux*.

She was, however, most agreeably mistaken;

no letter had arrived for his Lordship, and he
came to announce the necessity of delaying his
journey till the receipt of his English des-
patches.   Never did he pay a more welcome
visit, and seldom was news received with more
unfeigned satisfaction.   Perhaps, had he divined
the true cause of that satisfaction, he would
not only have been far less gratified, but would,
possibly, have actually departed without even
awaiting the arrival of the much-desired letters.
But there was something so pleasing in the
manner in which she alluded to the pleasure
which they should both have in hearing his
guitar, now that there were fewer claimants
on his time, and there was such an agreeable
absence of any kind friend to tell him that Mrs.
Lovaine was endeavouring to entrap him, that

he began also to rejoice at the unexpected circumstance, which promised him the means of enjoying her society a short time longer than he had originally expected or intended.

Under the present circumstances, Mrs. Lovaine did not wish to encourage Elinor's regrets for the departure of their friends, or at least, she hoped to prevent any danger to the success of her own views, arising from those regrets.

" How very, very dull, dear Mamma, we shall find this place, now every body we liked is gone !"

" Not every body, surely, my dear—the Lucas's and the Burtons, and Mr. Russell, and Mr. Charles Woodford, are still here, and I thought you liked some, if not all of them,

very much. You will still have plenty of part-
ners to dance with; Charlotte Lucas is a very
nice girl, and so is Mary Burton."

" Oh yes, Mamma, and I like them very
well in their different ways; but they cannot
make up for the loss of the De Cliffords."

" I was afraid, my love, you would feel the
loss of your young friend," replied Mrs. Lovaine: " she is almost the first great friend,
out of your own family, that you have had,
and I feared you would be low at parting
with her. However, I dare say we shall all
meet again soon, so do not make yourself very
unhappy about it."

" I am not unhappy—that is, I am not
really very unhappy, though I certainly am
very sorry that Emily is gone; indeed, I think

we shall miss them all sadly. Lady Harriet was always so good-natured to me; and Mr. De Clifford used to take us such nice rides; and when I first came here, and was not strong, he never would let me ride too far; just as if I had been his own daughter—he must be a very amiable man. I hope little Harry won't forget me; he and Mary are the nicest children I ever saw."

" They are very pretty and intelligent," said Mrs. Lovaine.

" I long to leave Spa now, Mamma! we shall have no fun, now they are all gone."

" Emily ought to be flattered, if she knew how much you regretted the loss of her society; I suspect she stands for the *all*."

Elinor slightly blushed, and without replying

U. OF ILL. LIB.

to this observation, proceeded to lament the absence of Mr. Mordaunt, and some others who had gone away that morning. Of William De Clifford alone she did not make individual mention; an omission which in some degree alarmed the prudent mind of Mrs. Lovaine. "I suppose," she said, "William De Clifford will take orders soon after his return to England," by way of introducing the subject into conversation. "He seems to be a very well disposed young man, though not over bright."

"Is he not clever?" asked Elinor, with some embarrassment, and much surprise; for she had always considered him as one of the cleverest men of the day.

"Oh no, my love! decidedly otherwise;

indeed, I believe that is the reason of his being
intended for the church.   Poor fellow ! I believe his prospects are not very good.   A poor
curacy will, I imagine, be his fate for some
time."

" Emily told me he was to have a family
living near them in the country."

" So I understood from Lady Harriet—but
not till the death of the present incumbent, a
healthy middle-aged man—and then it is only
about £300 a year."

Elinor did not know to the contrary, and
was silent.   " To be sure," continued Mrs.
Lovaine, " it is lucky that poor William De
Clifford is not attractive enough, for there to
be much risk of his inducing any girl of fashion
to share his poverty with him.   There is no

idea more mistaken, than supposing that the absurd romance of love in a cottage is more likely to be productive of happiness, because the cottage happens to be a parsonage; or to imagine that a clergyman by marrying, does not subject himself and his wife to as many privations as any other individual with a small income."

" But do you not think, Mamma, that a clergyman particularly requires the comfort of a wife, and that, indeed, a wife is often of great use to him in the fulfilment of his parish duties ?"

" Most decidedly I do, my dear; indeed, I think, as soon as it is possible for them to do so, it is highly expedient that a clergyman should marry. But the object of his choice should not be one who has been brought up in, and accustomed to all the splendour and comforts of rank and fortune. Much as I disapprove of *mésalliances* in general, yet I think a young man of family, without fortune, and in the church, should rather seek a wife from those who would gain, instead of lose, by the alliance. In my opinion, it is a most unprincipled thing in any man, to endeavour to induce a girl, by working upon her feelings, to share with him privations and discomforts, of which, from her former and happier condition, she can have formed no previous idea. That such men are, however, to be found, we have, alas, almost daily proof; and in their defence, youth and inexperience may sometimes be urged; but that parents should be found

willing to permit the sacrifice of their children's interest, does seem almost incredible.
I may have, and heaven knows have, many
faults,. but for indifference, or wanton neglect of my child's establishment, never, my
dear Elinor, shall you have to reproach
me."

There was a kindness, and a tone of maternal
affection in the wind-up of Mrs. Lovaine's
discourse upon the duty of parents opposing
their children's wishes, that touched Elinor's
feelings, and utterly prevented her detecting
any little fallacy in her mother's views, that
might otherwise have struck her. She remained for some few minutes in perfect silence,
as if absorbed in thought at what she had just
heard, till at last her colour heightened, her

bosom gently heaved, her eyes filled, and down her cheek stole fast the big round tears.

To say that she had seriously contemplated the prospect of one day performing, what Mrs. Lovaine was pleased to consider the romantic part of clergyman's wife, would be out-stepping the truth; but that when Emily had talked of her brother's pretty little parsonage, and the comforts of its vicinity to the paternal mansion, the thought had glanced across her mind of how pleasant such a residence must be, and of the delight of being able to hold daily intercourse with Emily, we will not deny. The opinions which had just been uttered by her mother, at once produced the recurrence of these thoughts, and at the same time the annihilation of whatever hopes might formerly have accompanied them. Her feelings had been a good deal excited within the last twenty-four hours, and, without being herself aware of the precise cause, she was now completely overcome.

" Come Elinor," said Mrs. Lovaine, " I see that the parting with your young friend has made you rather nervous; it is very natural: but we will change the subject, my love, and dismiss the De Cliffords, and our late gaieties, from our thoughts for the present.

Mrs. Lovaine was far, very far, from wishing to make her daughter unhappy. She was indeed bent upon her being otherwise, but she was also bent upon chusing herself the means to so desirable an end. In ascribing Elinor's emotion to her recent separation from

Emily, and the breaking-up of a very agreeable party, she certainly gave expression to her wishes, if not entirely to her belief Elinor willingly accepted, and soon even adopted her mother's solution of her agitation, and thus was Mrs. Lovaine's object in feigning ignorance of its true cause completely answered. The conversation soon took another turn; and the following morning Elinor resumed her usual occupations with her wonted composure.

Her thoughts may perchance have still dwelt on those who had lately formed and shared her pleasure; but this we have no right to judge, for she alluded not to them.

CHAPTER IV.

WE have already mentioned, that Lord Goldsborough was awaiting the arrival of letters
from England. That which he particularly
expected was from his solicitor on matters of
business; but he was also very anxious to receive accounts from home, allusions having been
made, in a short note from one of his sisters,
concerning an event respecting which, though
attaching no great importance to his information, he was in some degree interested. The
letter from the solicitor arrived by the post
three days after the departure of the De Clif-

fords, unaccompanied, however, by any from the noble house of Reading. Lord Goldsborough concluded, that as his sister had promised that he should hear again from home in the course of the week, the letter must have miscarried; and finding himself quite as well amused at Spa as he was likely to be elsewhere, he determined to await the arrival of another post, for the chance of receiving the expected despatch, before he went further afield in quest of pleasure, instruction, or whatever else he sought on the Continent.

Mrs. Lovaine was pleased at this delay; for though she could not so far deceive herself, as to fancy his attentions sufficiently directed to Elinor to justify, at present, any expectation of the fulfilment of her fondest hopes in that

quarter, yet she did flatter herself that by establishing an intimacy and a friendship with his
Lordship, she was in some degree advancing
the chance of their future completion; it was
with much regret, therefore, that she beheld
the arrival of that post day, beyond which he
had determined not to postpone his journey,
from the expectation of the family intelligence
before alluded to.

It so happened that at the moment when Mrs.
Lovaine's servant was sent to the post-office,
Lord Goldsborough was in the act of entering
her house. The servant informed him of his
errand, and asked whether he should procure
his Lordship's letters (if any) at the same time.
The offer was accepted, and ere long, letters
were placed in the hands of each of the trio.

Elinor's contained but a few hurried and affectionate lines from Miss De Clifford, informing her of their safe arrival at Brussels, and expressing the regrets of herself, and others of her party, at having quitted Spa. With this epistle, though short, Elinor was so much engrossed, that she was alike unconscious of the agitation betrayed in Lord Goldsborough's countenance, and of the anxiety with which her mother regarded him.

Mrs. Lovaine's letter was from her husband, and having hastily glanced over its contents, to ascertain that it was the bearer of no very particular intelligence, she cast her eyes towards Lord Goldsborough, who believing his companions to be equally engaged as himself, was at no

pains to conceal the various expressions of surprise and anger, which he felt, and very plainly
exhibited in his countenance, during the perusal of his letter. When he had finished
reading it, he continued to gaze in silence on
the paper, apparently lost in thought.

"All well at home, I trust," said Mrs. Lovaine, in her softest voice.

" Thank you, they are in very good health,"
was his Lordship's very laconic reply. Then
instantly rising from his chair, he took a hasty
leave, and quitted the apartment.

" What can be the matter! "exclaimed Mrs.
Lovaine, as soon as she heard his footsteps
audibly descending. " I am sure he has heard
something dreadful; I am almost sorry I did

not ask him the cause of his uneasiness; I am so afraid he should think my not having done so, unkind."

" He could not think that, dear Mamma, for you spoke to him in so kind a tone; I did not observe his countenance till you spoke, but it seemed to me that he looked more angry than unhappy as he left the room."

" Had I not known him to have possessed the best of tempers, I might also have been inclined to think so; but that cannot be. No! his feelings are very acute, and have, I fear, been much wounded by some intelligence conveyed in that letter."

Elinor, who pretended to no knowledge of Lord Goldsborough's character, had no observation to offer, even if her mother had given

her time to make one; but she was so occupied
in speculating upon the cause of her friend's
emotion, and its probable effects, that this
silence was unperceived, and Mrs. Lovaine
continued to give expression to her surmises at
short intervals.

" I wonder whether he will set off for England to night! I suppose he will, at any rate,
come and take leave of us before he goes! I
wonder which of his family wrote to him!
There can be no death in the family, because
he said they are all well; how very extraordinary! I should like to know what sort of
woman Lady Reading is! Perhaps one of his
sisters have run away. I shall leave word, when
we go to the ball to-night, that I shall be at
home very early, in case he should call. It

would be so vexatious to miss him, for perhaps he would then communicate the cause of the misery which I am sure he is now enduring!"

Although Elinor had not herself perceived any very particular indication of sadness in Lord Goldsborough, yet she now began almost to believe in its existence; and the idea of suffering in a fellow creature could not but be painful to one of her nature; and though she had never shared her mother's admiration of Lord Goldsborough, she warmly sympathized in her compassion for his unhappiness.

It was the night of one of the weekly balls at Spa, and thither, at the usual hour, repaired both mother and daughter. But what was their surprise on perceiving, a short time after they had entered the room, the folding-doors open to admit Lord Goldsborough!

There is something very disappointing in having one's tender sympathies unnecessarily aroused; and Elinor's newly acquired interest for a man whom she had pictured to herself as harassed and wretched, perplexed with painful doubts, or plunged in despair at some domestic calamity, vanished at once upon the reappearance of the composed, well-dressed, dignified heir-apparent. Mrs. Lovaine, too much impressed with her own conviction of his labouring under great affliction to be convinced of her error at once, even by his present air of perfect composure, prepared to receive him

with that *visage de circonstance*, so distressing
to those who are really afflicted, and so wholly
uncalled-for to those who are otherwise. Finding, however, that this said *visage de circonstance* was returned with no sad smile, reluc-
tantly dispelling for an instant a deep settled
gloom, but with his usual air of self-satisfaction,
and a simple observation upon the extraordinary thinness of the assembly, in consequence
of the numerous departures since the ball of
the preceding week; she also resumed her
usual manner.

The curiosity of Mrs. Lovaine, however, to
know the cause of what she still considered
Lord Goldsborough's extraordinary conduct at
her house in the morning, was not abated, and
after a few common-place remarks *de part et*

d'autre, she inquired whether he purposed leav-
ing Spa early the next morning.

" I do not intend going at all to-morrow,
and perhaps not for some days to come; my
plans, however, are not yet quite settled."

Mrs. Lovaine was surprised beyond measure,
and she assured him, with the utmost truth,
that she was sincerely glad to hear that they
were not so soon to lose him. No allusion,
however, was made to the cause of this change
of plan, or to the letter from England. To
Mrs. Lovaine, the whole affair was extremely
puzzling; to Elinor, who was now persuaded
that no melancholy event had occurred, it was
one of extreme indifference.

The information of Lord Goldsborough's
intention of remaining at Spa, was not the

only circumstance which was destined, that evening, to excite in Mrs. Lovaine the mixed feelings of pleasure and surprise; for the first time since their acquaintance, he twice honoured Elinor with his hand, as her partner in the dance—procured her shawl and cloak, when departing, and actually escorted her to the carriage.

The reply to Mrs. Lovaine's observation, " How very much you got on with Lord Goldsborough, to-night, my dear child! he really made himself quite particular with you!" showed how little consequence Elinor attached to this difference of manner. " Probably it was owing to there being but few other people there," was her simple manner

of accounting for what her mother considered
as such an important change.

The greater part of the following morning
was spent by Lord Goldsborough at Mrs.
Lovaine's; and here again, contrary to his
wonted custom, he addressed most of his conversation to Miss Lovaine; he also again alluded to the uncertainty of his plans, and that
in a tone of some importance. Hopes would
glance across Mrs. Lovaine's mind; but still
she thought the change so sudden, and his
conduct altogether so extraordinary, that she
did not venture to build much upon it.

Elinor was engaged to spend the evening
with a friend: Mrs. Lovaine, being somewhat
tired from the preceding night's amusement,

did not accompany her. Well was she compensated for the loss of whatever amusement she might have found elsewhere; had she been absent from home, she would not have been the happiest of women by two hours so soon.

Scarcely an hour had elapsed from the time when Elinor had quitted the house, when a letter was delivered to Mrs. Lovaine: she instantly recognized the hand-writing of Lord Goldsborough; it was evidently longer than an ordinary note, and the servant informed her that its bearer awaited an answer. It must therefore, she concluded, be of some importance. She hastily tore open the letter, and read as follows:

" My dear Mrs. Lovaine,

" You will, I have no doubt, be much
" surprised at the receipt of this letter; I can
" only trust that its purport will be a sufficient
" apology for its abruptness, in the eyes of so
" indulgent a friend as yourself.

" Had a favourable opportunity offered itself
" at your house this morning, it was my inten-
" tion to have made a verbal communication
" of those feelings which now induce me to
" address you in writing. But you were not
" alone, and I thought that requesting the
" favour of a private interview with you might
" be unnecessarily agitating, both to yourself
" and your amiable daughter.

" Family circumstances, of which it is use-

" less to trouble you with the detail, have
" induced me to comply with the wishes of
" my parents, in seriously reflecting upon the
" necessity of doing what they term *settling*
" *myself*, and on the happiness which is likely
" to accrue, to one in my situation, from the
" marriage state.

" The result of these reflections being in
" favour of matrimony, the present object of
" my letter is to solicit your kind interference
" in my behalf with Miss Lovaine. The gen-
" tleness of her disposition, and the excellence
" of the principles that have, I doubt not, been
" instilled into her mind, from her earliest in-
" fancy, cannot fail to ensure happiness to the
" man on whom she bestows her hand. Should
" it be my fate to be that fortunate in-

" dividual, I hope it is almost unnecessary to
" add, that there will be nothing wanting,
" in my power, to prove myself worthy of her
" choice.

" I have desired the bearer of this to await
" your answer, as upon that will, of course,
" depend my future plans. If, as my wishes
" bid me hope, you and your daughter are
" propitious, I shall pay my respects to my
" bride elect to-morrow, and delay my de-
" parture from Spa again another day. If not,
" as it would, I think, be more agreeable for
" all parties that we should not meet at pre-
" sent, I would commence my journey to Italy
" at sunrise. At the same time offering you
" both my sincere good wishes, and trusting
" to your generosity never to betray the feel-

" ings expressed in this letter, and which 'mis-
" taken hopes' of success have 'alone induced
" me to acknowledge,

        " Believe me,

           " Dear Mrs. Lovaine,

              " Yours sincerely and faithfully,

                  " GOLDSBOROUGH."

The agitation with which Mrs. Lovaine read this very unexpected proposal may be more easily imagined than described. Cold and presumptuous as were the terms in which Lord Goldsborough couched his declaration of love and admiration for her daughter, she saw in them nothing but what was ardent, considerate, and unpretending.

That she lost no time in replying to a letter which, to her, had been so productive of happiness, will be easily believed. She scarcely dared trust her senses—it was like a dream! She wrote with unusual rapidity, as if to assure herself of its truth. Her reply was short, but expressive of the gratitude of herself and her daughter for his handsome offer, with a full acceptance of the same.

To await the return of Elinor, ere she thus disposed of her hand and heart for life, never once occurred to Mrs. Lovaine; because the idea of her not being equally elated as herself, at the brilliant prospect now opened to her, had never presented itself to her mind. Nor was this unnatural, to one of Mrs. Lovaine's

feelings and opinions; had she even attempted
to reason upon the matter, she would probably
have acted in the same manner.

To have returned no answer by Lord Goldsborough's servant, would have appeared to her
impossible; and, on the other hand, to have
implied to him a doubt, which she did not
herself entertain, of her daughter's ready ac-
quiescence, by not at once accepting for her the
proffered alliance, would have been considered
by her needlessly ungracious and unkind.

At a later hour than Mrs. Lovaine expected,
Elinor returned. They had been amusing
themselves with "*petits jeux*," of various kinds,
at the house where she had spent the evening,
and little did she expect, as she entered the
room, intending to detail to her mother the

trivial occurrences of the evening, the important communication that awaited her. Not a
moment was lost by Mrs. Lovaine in beginning
the subject. She read to her Lord Goldsborough's letter; told her of the answer she
had sent him; lauded him in the most rapturous terms; and spoke of her own extacies at
the fulfilment of what she now owned had been
her long-cherished hopes; till at last, wound
up to the highest pitch of excitement, she burst
into tears, threw her arms round Elinor's neck,
and thanked her for thus being the means of
affording her greater happiness than she had
ever experienced before.

Poor Elinor's surprise for a time rendered
her, as it were, drunk or bewildered. She returned her mother's caresses, and soon caught

the infection of her tears, if not of her joy.
Why she was thanked she scarcely knew:
for, certainly, anxious as she always was to
please her mother, she had not, in this instance, been given the option of doing otherwise. She at last sobbed out, " But you know,
dear Mamma, that Papa has never seen Lord
Goldsborough, and perhaps he may not give
his consent."

Now, although the circumstance of Mr. Lovaine not being personally acquainted with
another individual, had been urged as a conclusive objection against his becoming his son-
in-law, yet, in the present instance, it seemed
to have lost all its weight, for Mrs. Lovaine
replied,

" Do not be uneasy upon that score, my

love! It will, I know, give him as much pleasure as it does me, to see you united to such a
man as Lord Goldsborough."

Elinor continued to weep, notwithstanding
this consolatory assurance.

" I do not wonder," said Mrs. Lovaine, " at
your being so much overcome. There is no
case in which the extremes appear to meet
more than in the effects of excessive joy and
excessive grief. How well do I remember, that,
when my own marriage with your father, to
whom I had been long and devotedly attached,
was arranged, I was in such a state of nerves,
that those around me actually believed, at first,
that I was doing violence to my feelings in accepting him. It was, indeed, some days ere I
was sufficiently composed to enjoy the good

fortune that awaited me; and so, my dear, it will, I have no doubt, be with you. You must expect this nervousness; a good night's rest will be of great service to you; so, go to bed—dream of Lord Goldsborough—and receive him as he deserves when he comes to-morrow morning."

Elinor most willingly retired to bed, and would also willingly have retired to rest, could she have done so. She, however, slept but very little, and that little was much disturbed by fanciful dreams. At one time, whilst listening to the vows and protestations of Lord Goldsborough, she suddenly perceived that his face and figure was that of William De Clifford; at another, Lord Goldsborough was going to take orders, and she was presented to Lady Reading,

whom she found to be no other than her friend
Emily, grown to a gigantic height; again, she
thought herself at home, and heard her father
and mother disagreeing, she knew not on what
subject, till she distinctly heard Mr. Lovaine
say, " Elinor shall never marry at all, by my
consent." It was not till late in the morning
that she fell into a sound sleep, from which she
was aroused by a summons from her mother to
come down instantly into the drawing-room,
which she obeyed with all posssible despatch.

- " My dear girl," said Mrs. Lovaine, as she
entered the room, " I am sorry to have disturbed your sleep, but I knew that neither you
or Lord Goldsborough would forgive me if
you were not ready to receive him when he
called."

Elinor made no reply. In due time his
Lordship arrived. Mrs. Lovaine received him
with the cordiality and pleasure which she
really felt. Elinor was polite, but subdued
and embarrassed. Lord Goldsborough appeared self-satisfied, and was as much at his
ease as it was his nature to be; made signifi-
cant allusions to the event that he trusted
would take place in a few months; and regretted, though in a tone of most philosophical
contentment, that a long-standing promise to
travel in the north of Italy, with an old College friend, obliged him to delay his, and he
hoped he might, without presumption, say,
their mutual happiness.

Elinor blushed, but was relieved from the
necessity of making any reply to this lover-like

speech, by Mrs. Lovaine inquiring how soon he expected to return to England.

" I cannot be quite certain, yet ; but I hope I do not ask too much, in expressing my wish, that my future mother-in-law may be kind enough both to write herself, and to allow me, from time to time, to remind her of my existence," was the gracious reply to this question ; and his Lordship looked far more as if he had conferred, than requested, a favour.

The moment of his departure was one of considerable relief to Elinor. Mrs. Lovaine, dreading lest her daughter's embarrassment should have created in the mind of Lord Goldsborough any unpleasant suspicion of a want of attachment on her part, quitted the apartment with him, and said, in a confidential tone, " My poor child is so overcome by her present situation, that she scarcely knows what she says or does; but, my dear Lord Goldsborough, it is very natural; at her age the feelings are generally stronger, or at any rate, less under control, than at any other. I really believe she has wept for joy ever since the arrival of your kind letter last night. You will, I am sure, find in her a most amiable and affectionate companion; and, young as she is, I flatter myself that I may add with truth, that she has received an education, calculated at once to steady her conduct, and render her fit to fulfil the duties of a far more splendid situation than that in which she has been hitherto placed."

That Elinor should be so overpowered with

delight did not surprise Lord Goldsborough;
for to that circumstance he had in his own
mind attributed a manner, which to a more
sensitive lover would have been very far from
satisfactory; and he took his leave with feelings alike undisturbed by unpleasant suspicions and unavailing regrets at being thus
separated from his mistress, within a few hours
from the time of his becoming her accepted
admirer.

To Elinor's mind, the respite that was granted
in consequence of his Lordship's previous engagement to travel with a friend, afforded great
repose. She began to ask herself whether,
amongst her acquaintances, there was any one
she liked better than Lord Goldsborough. Her
heart whispered, for a moment, something in

favour of William De Clifford; but the thought was accompanied by the recollection of the very decided opinions expressed by Mrs. Lovaine against the marriage of needy clergymen: they had left no doubt upon her mind of the impossibility of her ever consenting to such an alliance for her own daughter; and to marry without the consent of both her parents never occurred to the single-minded Elinor as coming within the pale of possibility. Moreover, the said William had never expressed any preference for her; and she felt that he ought, at once, to be dismissed from her mind. She did not, however, forget that he had once appeared to think, when speaking of his sister's feelings towards Mr. Gordon, that our powers of liking and disliking were greatly under our control; and she flattered herself, that by endeavouring to think of Lord Goldsborough as her mother wished, he would become an object of less indifference, if not of repugnance to her, than he now was, before the time when she would be called upon to love, cherish, and obey him.

Whether unconsciously to herself, a hope that her fate was not yet quite irrevocably fixed —a hope, which the lapse of time that was to take place before they would again meet, might, not unnaturally, suggest, contributed to tranquillize her mind, we do not pretend to assert. We think it probable; but can only be certain of the fact, that although she was less cheerful than before she was the destined bride of Lord Goldsborough, she became much less agitated a few days after his departure, than she had been on that on which she had to receive him as the chosen means of her future happiness.

CHAPTER V.

WHILST Lord Goldsborough and his friend, (whom, according to agreement, he met at Brussels,) are crossing the Alps, and Mrs. Lovaine and her daughter paying bills, packing up, &c. &c., previous to their return home, we will beg leave to anticipate their return, and acquaint our readers, to the best of our power, with the thoughts, words, and deeds of all those whom we quitted some time ago, beginning from the period at which we took leave of them.

That Herbert was a little surprised at the

favourable impression made on his uncle by
Mr. Benson during their second interview, we
have already mentiond; nor was his surprise
diminished at finding, from the repeated mention of Mr. Benson's name by Mr. Lovaine,
that this favourable impression increased upon
further acquaintance, and that their intercourse became more frequent. Mr. Benson,
on the other hand, seldom alluded to Mr.
Lovaine in the presence of Herbert; a circumstance which astonished him less than it
might have otherwise done, because he at
once attributed this silence to his friend's forbearance, in not attacking the antiquated no-
tions and illiberal prejudices of his misjudging
relative.

The business which had occasioned Mr.

Lovaine's visit to the Metropolis detained him longer than he had at first expected, nor was he, perhaps, in his heart, sorry to have a fair excuse, without compromising his professed opinions in favour of the superiority of a country over a town life, thus to beguile the time which was still destined to elapse before the return of his wife and daughter should again release him from a solitude, of which he was far more heartily tired than he cared to own to himself, and still much less to others.

The frequency of Herbert's and of Mr. Benson's visits to Russell Square did not diminish, but as they seldom happened to meet there, each, for a time, supposed the other to have found less than former pleasure in the society of Mrs. Lawlie.

Our readers may remember, that she had appointed Mr. Benson for the morning following that dinner, at which the two friends had met at her house (of which we have before given the particulars) in order that he might resume his office of instructor, from which he had lately seceded; imagining, as he candidly told her, that he had been mistaken, in supposing her to be sufficiently above the general weaknesses of her sex, properly to appreciate the value of rational pursuits.

Considering Mr. Benson's professed inexperience in the characters of women, it must be confessed that this observation proved, by its instant effect, a wonderful knowledge, if not of woman-nature in general, yet most cer-

tainly of that of Mrs. Lawlie in particular.—
The idea of being lowered in the estimation of
a man who had looked upon her as the one
brilliant exception to her whole race, was one
she could not brook.   She had thought herself sufficiently secure of his good opinion, to
be able to devote her attention with impunity
to the acquisition of a new proselyte; but finding that his devotion was not yet proof against
neglect, she determined to divide her time and
attentions with more equality between Messrs.
Benson and Lovaine. With the former, therefore, she read and conversed in the morning
when alone; to the latter she was all smiles
and devotion at her evening *côteries,* where she
was secretly envied by those around her, for

her intimacy with one of such pretensions to rank, fashion, and fortune, as Herbert at once possessed and despised.

Of the existence of this little arrangement neither were aware: indeed, as they seldom happened to meet there, each imagined that the other had ceased to frequent the house. That there were little inconsistencies in the character of Mr. Benson, Herbert had had reason (as we mentioned at the close of a former chapter) to remark and discrimination enough to discover; and it was to some trifling and unimportant caprice that he attributed both the disinclination, which he had of late perceived in his friend to enter into any conversation relating to Mrs. Lawlie, and the supposed diminution of his visits to Russell

Square. The perception, however, that the
topic had ceased to be one of interest to Mr.
Benson, was sufficient reason for its non-intro-
duction by Herbert. Mr. Benson, on the
other hand, knowing the influence he possessed over the taste and mind of young Lovaine,
flattered himself that he would soon cease to
seek one who was no longer praised by himself,
and who, he justly believed, was originally
sought, solely on his own recommendation;
nor did he fail to attribute to this cause the
change, which, from Herbert's silence, he believed to have taken place in his feelings towards Mrs. Lawlie.

Perhaps the lady herself was not quite unconscious of the erroneous conclusion to which
her two friends had arrived, respecting the

quantum of intercourse which she maintained
with each : but as it was very apparent that
each was satisfied, she thought, in the bene-
volence of her heart, that it was prudent and
wise to let them have the benefit of the only
ignorance that could be productive of bliss.

Mr. Lawlie was unfortunately sometimes a
blunderer, though, to be sure, poor man! as
he could not reckon with as much precision
the thoughts and motives which actuated his
wife's conduct, as he could calculate the probable loss or profit upon rums and sugars, it was
no great wonder that he should sometimes
enact the part of Marplot with wonderful and
unconscious success.

It was very seldom that Mr. Lawlie had
time to interrupt his lady's education during

the morning, and he was perfectly satisfied, so long as things went on well in the counting-house, and that he found her disposed to treat him with the courtesy which he thought his due as a husband; though he was by no means blind to that inferiority in point of acquirement and talent, with which his dear Maria never failed, in the most delicate manner, to impress him.

It chanced one morning, that just as Mr. Benson was in the middle of an elaborate and really very able analysis of a pamphlet recently published on the Paper Currency, Mr. Lawlie put his head in at the door, and addressing his wife, said: "Maria, my dear, I have just met Lovaine, who begged me, in answer to your note, to tell you that he should be most happy to dine with us to-day, and to take my place at the play, for I expect a gentleman here to-night on business; and as he is to sail to-morrow, I cannot put him off." Then, with a sort of nod, that meant to say, "Do not let me interrupt you," he closed the door, and retired.

He did interrupt them, however, and that most effectually; for never did the analysis, so well begun, come to a conclusion. For a few minutes both remained silent, and there was about Mr. Benson's countenance that peculiar expression which we have before mentioned, and which nothing but the constant assurance on his own part, that he scorned the influence of passion, could have prevented from being mistaken for one of extreme wrath.

From whatever cause it arose, it had the effect of decidedly embarrassing Mrs. Lawlie, who was however the first to break the silence, by saying, " I suppose you are too much occupied to join us also to-night?   I hardly liked to propose it to you, for I know that that sort of dissipation is still less in your line than in mine. I feel it is a weakness: but to see one of Shakespeare's plays well acted does afford me a little pleasure for the moment; it is an agreeable recreation, after graver and more worthy pursuits."

Whether Mr. Benson thought the apology for being amused at one of the highest treats that can be afforded to the man of taste and feeling, sufficient to justify his going, we know not, for to that character he was not wont to

plead guilty; but certain it is that he accepted the invitation, coldly, and the theatre was
that night honoured with his presence, in company with Mrs. Lawlie and her party.

Herbert Lovaine was rather surprised, but
by no means displeased at this rencontre. He
considered the presence of Mr. Benson at all
times a sort of agreeable sanction to whatever
amusements they partook of together, and he
was also glad to perceive that the admiration
with which his monitor had at first inspired
him, by description, for the talents of Mrs.
Lawlie; had not yet subsided into the indifference and contempt which he usually expressed for female society, for he never quitted
her side during the whole of that evening.

Herbert was glad to be neither obliged to

accuse his friend 'of inconsistency, or himself of frivolity, in being too easily pleased, and from this time his reserve respecting his visits to Russell Square wore off sufficiently for him to mention, occasionally, his being engaged to dine or pass the evening there; to allude to some new light whose acquaintance he had made there; to say that, in short, which proved to Mr. Benson that his intercourse with the house was more frequent than he had imagined previous to their meeting at the play, and more than was perfectly agreeable to the composure of his own mind.

And why was it not agreeable, our inquisitive readers may be inclined to ask: but to that we must decline giving any positive answer. The power of the tender passions was so wholly denied by Mr. Benson, that we dare not at present attribute any thing in him to their influence. How far he was justified in this denial we shall leave to the judgment of our readers to decide at the close of our narrative —it is not our business to prejudge.

Mr. Benson had occasionally remarked, that whenever the name of Lawlie was mentioned in the presence of Mr. Lovaine senior, it was received with some marks of impatience to be rid of the topic; it was, in fact, one on which he had made himself ridiculous, by mistaken and over positiveness; and he, not unnaturally, disliked to be reminded of that extraordinary fact, *viz.* his being mistaken.

Mr. Benson knew not the cause of this impatience. His curiosity, however, being piqued to ascertain from whence it arose, he took the opportunity of Mr. Lovaine's inquiring of him if he knew where Herbert dined that day, to introduce the subject.

" I suppose, as usual, Sir, at Mr. and Mrs. Lawlie's," was the reply.

Mr. Lovaine made no remark.

" Are you acquainted, Sir, with your ne-phew's friends in Russell Square?" continued Mr. Benson.

" Never saw them in my life—know nothing about them."

" You must surely have often heard them mentioned by Herbert; I wonder indeed that he has not persuaded you to make their ac-quaintance."

" I am too old to be seeking new acquaintance, thank you—very well if they come in my way; and Herbert knows me better than to be always talking to me about people that I neither know or care for."

" It must be mortifying to your nephew, to be debarred from talking of those with whom he lives on such terms of intimacy. Mrs. Lawlie is a remarkable woman," he continued, hoping to arouse some interest on the part of his companion.

" More fool she—I hate remarkable women ! what business have they to be remarkable?"

That was a question to which Mr. Benson had too much respect for the prejudices of his elder to offer any reply.

" You do her injustice in calling her a fool, Sir; I should not think, to judge by appear-

ances, · that that opinion can be founded on
Herbert's estimation of her abilities."

" I am not very apt, I can assure you,
Mr. Benson, to found my opinion on any
man's judgment but my own; and I am certainly still less likely to be influenced by the
whims and caprices which a boy of his age
dignifies with the name of opinions."

Mr. Benson was too well-bred to shew
Mr. Lovaine the folly of his dogma, but said,
" I hope you will not mortify Herbert by the
expression of any unfavourable opinion of
Mrs. Lawlie; it would, I am sure, be very
painful to him."

Mr. Lovaine speedily turned the conversation; he almost feared that Mr. Benson knew
of the dispute which had already arisen be-

tween him and his nephew on the subject.   In
that, however, he was much mistaken; as was
Mr. Benson in the thought to which the tes-
tiness of Mr. Lovaine's manner had given rise,
viz. that he suspected with displeasure that
Herbert was a victim to the fascination of the
lady in question. *Perhaps* " his wish was father
to that thought!" But we have before made
known our intention of confining ourselves to
the relation of facts, without professing to
guess at motives.

CHAPTER VI.

MR. BENSON's remarks had not fallen wholly
without effect on the ears of Mr. Lovaine; he
was convinced, upon reflection, that they had
not been made unintentionally, and his curiosity
was aroused to ascertain their meaning.   The
more he thought on what had passed, the more
his misgiving of his nephew having informed
Mr. Benson of his blunder was strengthened,
and he was determined to take the first opportunity of discovering from Herbert, without
appearing to do so, the truth or falsehood of
of this idea.

" Has Mr. Lawlie made much money, Herbert?" inquired Mr. Lovaine, in a tone of perfect *insouciance,* a few days after his last interview with Mr. Benson, by way of introducing the subject.

- Herbert did not know, and said so.

" Do they maintain a large establishment? The *Parvenu* merchants of the present day generally beat the old established families in point of display, if not in good taste."

" There is nothing ostentatious in Mr. and Mrs. Lawlie's establishment; he is very much occupied and interested in his business, and she is quite above deriving pleasure from so empty a source as the useless display of their well-earned riches," was Herbert's reply, and the conversation would have been in danger of dropping, had not Mr. Lovaine began upon a fresh tack.

" Mr. Benson is acquainted with the Lawlies, is he not? I have occasionally heard him mention their names."

" He knows them intimately, and indeed he was the person who introduced me to their acquaintance."

" I wish he had done no such thing," muttered Mr. Lovaine to himself. " I say, Herbert," continued he out loud, and in a jocular tone of voice, " do you remember my blunder about Miss Lawlie? The old boy was a little dunny that day, I suppose you think—did Benson know of your *marriage* with *Miss Lawlie*—hey?"

Herbert smiled at his uncle's way of alluding

to the ridiculous error into which he had been
led by his hasty prejudices, and assured him
that Mr. Benson was quite ignorant of there
having been any such report.

" It must be very flattering to the old lady to
have you youngsters always seeking her society," remarked Mr. Lovaine.

" What old lady, sir?"

" Old Mrs. Lawlie, to be sure·"

" She is dead, my dear uncle; they were
in mourning for her soon after I became acquainted with the family."

Mr. Lovaine had, in his confusion at finding that Herbert's affections were engaged to
no young lady of the name or family of Lawlie, concluded, with an equally erroneous haste,
that there was nothing young belonging to

them; he was, therefore, as much surprised at this reply, as if he had always heard the individual in question designated as *old*.

" Pray, what age then is Mrs. Lawlie?" he asked, as if the difference of opinion could only be caused by their affixing that unpleasant adjective to different periods in the human existence.

" She is about two or three and thirty, I believe, Sir; but she scarcely looks as much."

" Is it possible! I was persuaded that you had told me she was both old and ugly."

" Believe me, Sir, she is as far from one as the other. Mrs. Lawlie is still young, and is generally considered handsome; indeed she is decidedly so in my opinion."

For once in his life, Mr. Lovaine preserved

a prudent silence upon the receipt of this information. He seemed fated to be mistaken in whatever he said or thought concerning her; he, therefore, carefully abstained from the slightest allusion to a fresh idea, which at that moment crossed his mind upon the subject.

Neither spoke for a few minutes; but Mr. Lovaine luckily remembering then, that he had got a letter in the adjoining room for his nephew, very obligingly volunteered fetching it, and thus got rid of the topic.

The letter was from Elinor, and written not very long after their arrival at Spa. Herbert and Elinor had been brought up as brother and sister, and were much attached to each other. The difference in their age had been too great as children, for them to be quite

playfellows, but he had always treated her
his favourite plaything, and she had always
looked up to him with the love and respect
due to a brother, and an elder.

Changed as he was in many of his pursuits,
habits, and feelings, he had never altered in
his affection for her. Perhaps he hoped that
she was sufficiently young and ductile to be
benefited by his wisdom and instruction; be
that as it might, certain it was that he continued the habit.of sacrificing some of his
precious time to maintaining a correspondence
with her; and that the receipt of her letters
was generally to him a circumstance of pleasure
and satisfaction.

To this general rule, however, the perusal
of the epistle in question appeared to form the

exception. Herbert read it attentively, but his countenance was far from indicative of his having received pleasure from its contents; indeed we fear, that had a skilful physiognomist observed the lines of his countenance as he refolded the letter, he might, with truth, have been taxed with the betrayal of decided ill-humour.

" Thank heaven ! Elinor seems to be quite recovered, by her mother's account. to me. Does she speak of her own health to you ?" said Mr. Lovaine, who did not at first perceive that Herbert's brow was somewhat clouded.

" She says she is very well, Sir; but I should imagine that she was very unlikely to continue so."

" Good God! what do you mean? Has
any thing happened?" eagerly inquired the
affectionate father.

" Nothing, Sir, at present; but she appears
to be living in a round of unwholesome dissipation, and frivolous excitement, that must be
as bad for her mind, as dangerous to her
health."

" That sounds more like the fears of a man
of my time of life than of yours, Herbert!
You really alarmed me at first; I thought you
had some bad news, and you looked so confoundedly black over the dear child's letter,
that I apprehended you had some greater
cause of annoyance, than that of hearing that a
girl of her age was amusing herself like her
cotemporaries. I hope she will not do more

than her strength will bear; but for my part, I
like to hear of young people being gay. I suppose it is one of the steps in the march of
intellect to avoid being young, and to hold in
contempt all the gaiety which the very birds
and beasts instinctively feel in Spring. If you
want to moralize upon the waste of time at a
ball—upon the abuse of talent in the pursuit
of foxes, hares, &c.—the folly of shooting—the
worthlessness of society—the, the—in short all
upon which you ever do moralize, go to your
Russell Square friends; I dare say they will
enter into the merit of your observations much
more than I shall; and pray remember, that I
beg of you not to endeavour to persuade my
own darling Elinor to be an old woman before
she is a young one.".

" My Russell Square friends, as you are
pleased to designate Mr. and Mrs. Lawlie,
Sir, require no advice of mine; and, least of
all, upon such a subject. You will, of course,
be guided by your own opinions as to the conduct of Elinor's education; and I trust she
may escape from the dangerous contamination
of idleness and frivolity with which she is now
surrounded, and from which no woman, in my
opinion, ever does escape with impunity. It
is, however, hardly probable, and the less so,
as she seems equally captivated at present by
worthless pursuits and their pursuers."

At whom this attack was levelled, Mr. Lovaine knew not; but he was extremely displeased at the sentiments expressed by Herbert, and the tone in which they were deliver-

ed. A few more dictatorial speeches on his part, and some sharp replies on that of Herbert, closed the morning's interview, and they separated with mutual feelings of dissatisfaction.

Had Mr. Lovaine watched his nephew's countenance, he would have perceived that it was in the perusal of the second page of his daughter's letter that its serenity was first disturbed; and if he had seen the letter, he would have found in that page the following passage :—

" The more I see of Emily De Clifford, the better I like her. She says she knew you a little in London last year. I wish you had known her well, and liked her as much as I do; for I am sure that, in that case, you would have tried to marry her: and now, if you were to be ever so much inclined, it would, I fear, be too late.   There is here a Mr. Gordon, Lord Melrose's eldest son, who, every one says, is extremely in love with her; He is always with the De Cliffords; and I heard to-day, from a person who is intimate with the two parties concerned, that both Emily's and Mr. Gordon's parents wish for the marriage."

Why this simple piece of information should have produced upon its reader such unpleasant effects, we must leave at present to the ingenuity of our readers to discover.   That it was the cause of those effects was, however, most true—the *pourquoi du pourquoi* time perhaps will shew.

Herbert spent his evening at Mrs. Lawlie's.

Never could the injustice of the charge of age and ugliness, preferred against her in the morning by his uncle, have appeared more utterly groundless. She happened to be dressed in an unusually becoming manner, a circumstance which, of course, much heightened her natural good looks; and although Herbert was of too philosophical a turn of mind to be attracted by so trifling an occurrence, yet the more glaring appeared the injustice done her, the more an object of interest did she immediately become in his eyes.

Nor did Mrs. Lawlie fail to gain in the comparison which, voluntarily or involuntarily, was instituted in Herbert's mind between her, and those with whom he had learnt in the morning that his cousin was, with so much pleasure, as-

sociating at Spa. He never had thought Mrs.
Lawlie so intellectual, or her pursuits so rational, as when he recollected the contents of
that letter, and the discussion that had arisen,
in consequence, between himself and his
uncle.

CHAPTER VII.

THE result of the little altercation detailed
in our last chapter, was far from producing in
Mr. Lovaine, senior, any increase of good-
will towards Mrs. Lawlie, similar to that felt
by Mr. Lovaine, junior. A suspicion that his
nephew's pleasure in the lady's society arose
from what he considered a far more natural
and accountable predilection in her favour,
than that of a mere wish to improve himself
by the discussion and cultivation of literary
and political subjects, had instantly glanced
across his mind, when first the surprising fact

of her being neither old or ugly, had been disclosed to him.

This suspicion had strengthend upon reflection; nor was it unmixed with feelings of displeasure, at being what he considered the dupe of his nephew's wilful deception. He looked upon his denial of the attachment to the imaginary Miss Lawlie, with which he had formerly taxed him, as no better than an equivocation; that he had merely cleared himself upon a quibble; and that he had affected to be unjustly accused, when, in fact, the only injustice done him, was in the over-mildness of the accusation. In short, that he had made him appear, and almost confess himself in the wrong, when in point of fact he had been, as usual, quite in the right.

These were heavy counts against poor Herbert; and they acquired as much force when they had been conned over in Mr. Lovaine's own mind only, as if they had, from good evidence, received " confirmation strong as proofs of holy writ," of their justice and truth.

It was under these new and unpleasant impressions, that Mr. Lovaine accidentally met Mr. Benson. He disliked being alone, and therefore, with feelings very different from those which first induced him to ask Mr. Benson, as a peace-offering to Herbert, he now invited him to dine, and pass those hours in his company, which Herbert was spending in that of Mrs. Lawlie; and when, it must be confessed, that his feelings went nearer to justify his uncle's suspicions than they had ever done before, or perchance might ever have done, but for the trifling events of the morning.

It was not in Mr. Lovaine's disposition to be reserved, and more particularly was he disposed to be otherwise, when his curiosity was aroused or his anger excited. In the present instance, therefore, as might be expected, he was far from inclined to withhold his opinions. His impression of Mr. Benson's character had continued unaltered since the day of his first dinner; nor, indeed, had Mr. Benson ever given him reason to change it; for he had uniformly persevered in the same prudent and inoffensive course which he had on that day adopted, of abstaining from the expression of such principles and opinions as would have been incomprehensible and revolting to the darkened mind of a country gentleman, nursed in the long-established prejudices of a monopolizing aristocracy. Had he ever recommended a similar forbearance to his friend Herbert, how much better would it have been for all parties.

Mr. Lovaine, as may be remembered, considered it an advantage to his nephew to have formed a friendship with one a few years older (which, in his opinion, was always synonymous with a few degrees wiser) than himself. In addition, therefore, to his natural inclination to communicate to others whatever disturbed his own mind, he looked to Mr. Benson for assistance in making Herbert sensible of his misconduct towards himself, and to reclaim him from what he considered his evil ways.

No sooner, therefore, was the cloth removed and the servants dismissed from the dining-room, than the subject of Herbert's profound admiration for Mrs. Lawlie was brought on the *tapis.*

Mr. Lovaine had a willing auditor, for the matter was by no means one of indifference to Mr. Benson.

" That boy has shamefully deceived me," said Mr. Lovaine. " Some time ago I taxed him with a preference for Miss Lawlie, imagining that it was for her charms that he had quitted the country at a much earlier period than he was wont to do, and altered all his habits and pursuits in life. He refuted the charge with a degree of warmth which was inexcusable, considering our relative positions, and which could only be palliated by the supposition of his complete innocence, and my consequent injustice. He repelled, with unblushing effrontery, the idea of engaging himself to Miss Lawlie, adducing in his defence the conclusive argument that, to his knowledge, no such person existed: but it was nothing better than an equivocation; knowing, as he did, that my mistake only consisted in having called the object of his attention *Miss,* instead of *Mrs.* Lawlie, and that I had given him credit for an attachment, honourable at least towards its object, instead of disgraceful to himself, and degrading to her."

" Since when, Sir, have you discovered this
cause of displeasure with my friend?"

" I never knew it till this morning; but I
have no doubt on the subject now, unless you
can as positively prove to me the lady's non-
existence, as did Herbert that of Miss Lawlie."   ı

" That, Sir, truth will not permit: of her
existence there is no more doubt, than of
Herbert's frequent visits to her house."

" And she is young and handsome?"

" Of her beauty I profess myself to be no
judge; but I have heard those who regard
external appearances consider her so; and indeed I remember to have once heard Herbert
himself say that he thought her handsome.
That she is superior in intellect to her sex in

general I have very little doubt; and of her youth I have none, for she accidentally mentioned her age in my presence the other day."

That Mr. Benson was no admirer of the fair sex did not escape Mr. Lovaine; but he willingly forgave him at that moment for any little want of gallantry in his opinions or expressions, thinking that the less he was disposed to be swayed by female influence, the more he was likely to prove useful to himself.

" You speak of beauty with a degree of philosophy that is, to say the least, unusual at your time of life. Would to Heaven you could mould this scapegrace nephew of mine a little more after your fashion." (Mr. Lovaine had no idea with how much success he had already done so.) " I am determined to put a stop to his dangling any longer after petticoat pedants; and I am sure Mr. Benson that, as his friend, you will not refuse me your assistance in effecting so very desirable an object."

" Petticoat pedant," would have grated a good deal on Mr. Benson's ears had it not been for the conclusion of this speech; but the prospect of being rid of the constant visits of his disciple, where he always considered him *de trop*, sweetened the bitterness of the impertinent epithet.

The conversation upon a subject so highly interesting to both parties was not likely to be soon dropped. Mr. Lovaine appealed to Mr. Benson's own observations as to the existence of Herbert's preference for Mrs. Lawlie. Mr.

Benson did not deny it; nor did he omit
to mention how often, and how strongly he
had advised him to devote his mind to useful
pursuits, and to forswear the influence of that
most unreasonable of all passions—love.

What Mr. Benson considered to be useful
pursuits, he did not state to Mr. Lovaine; but
as there was nothing to be said against useful
pursuits in the abstract, and as Mr. Lovaine
was highly impressed at the moment with the
superior good sense of Mr. Benson, because he
was of the same opinion as himself, he was
not disposed to cavil at any thing uttered by
him.

Had poor Herbert talked to his uncle of
following the advice which Mr. Benson owned
to having given him; had he declared his de-

votion to the pursuit of useful learning, and
openly forsworn all pretension to the softer passions, as dangerous, or, to say the least, unworthy of a reasonable being, Mr. Lovaine would
have treated him and his professions with that
contempt with which he was wont to treat what
he regarded as the unbecoming assumption of
one, too young to judge for himself. But Mr.
Benson perfectly agreed with him in the expediency of preventing the frequency, if not
the continuance, of Herbert's intercourse with
that family, to which he had himself so un-
wisely introduced him: ergo, Mr. Benson was
a very sensible, modest young man in Mr. Lovaine's eyes, and all he said was well received;
and thus did Mr. Benson fan the flame of
wrath against one, who had never yet har-

boured a feeling of jealousy, or an evil thought of any kind, towards himself.

Mr. Benson, notwithstanding this conversation, was not guilty of premeditated treachery; perhaps, indeed, if Mr. Lovaine had merely questioned him as to the fact of his nephew's being in love with Mrs. Lawlie, he would not have felt himself justified in asserting its truth upon grounds no better than apprehensions; or in sowing dissentions upon a bare suspicion, between his friend and the person to whom that friend owed, and from whom he expected every worldly good; but the positive manner in which Mr. Lovaine asserted that, which Mr. Benson had hitherto but apprehended, aroused those feelings which Herbert knew not that his friend possessed. The bane and antidote were held out together; for if his peace was poisoned by Mr. Lovaine's communication, he instantly saw the remedy in the angry exercise of a guardian's authority. The temptation was too great to be resisted; and ere he and Mr. Lovaine separated on that evening, he had consented to be the reporter, not to say the spy, of Herbert's actions.

It was agreed that Mr. Lovaine should not allude to the subject of Mrs. Lawlie to his nephew till Mr. Benson thought it advisable for him so to do, and that, above all, Mr. Benson's name shonld never be mentioned, as having taken part in saving him from the dangers into which he was now so blindly running; for grateful as in time Herbert must, and would feel to those who had preserved him from the disgraceful consequences of an illegal attachment, it was better that he should feel that gratitude to his uncle only; for, in fact, to him alone would it be owing; none other had a right to interfere; and if Mr. Benson acted under his directions with any success, he was but the instrument, and deserved not the praise due to his director.

Mr. Lovaine was perfectly captivated with his companion; "it is indeed," thought he to himself, "a long long while since I have met with a young man, who united at once such ability, discernment, candour, and disinterestedness! Could I but live to see Herbert resemble him, I should close my eyes upon this life with the satisfaction of feeling that I was placing my family and fortune in the hands of one well worthy of the trust."

We really believe that so entirely was Mr. Lovaine prejudiced at that moment in favour of Mr. Benson, that he might have almost hinted with safety, that abuse in old and public institutions did sometimes exist, and that it would be well to reform them. He, however, offered no such hint. To find himself the confidential friend of a man of Mr. Lovaine's family and *calibre* in the world, could not but be gratifying to a character such as we have described Mr. Benson's to be; and he was too acute not to perceive that, until his footing was still more secure, it would be unsafe to broach those opinions, which would tend as much to lower him in the estimation of Mr. Lovaine, as they had raised him in that of his own little band of devoted followers.

Mr. Lovaine having promised to refrain from the expression of his displeasure to Herbert till Mr. Benson should deem a measure of that sort to be advisable, had, on his part, received assurances that no time should be lost in discovering the state both of Herbert's and Mrs. Lawlie's feelings towards each other. They accordingly agreed to meet again, so soon as it had been in Mr. Benson's power to obtain the desired information; and when they parted, it was with that mutual good-will which confederates, either for good or evil, seldom fail to entertain for each other, when no difference of opinion as to the means of obtaining the end desired has disturbed their union.

That Mr. Benson should lose no time in beginning his operations, by introducing the mention of Herbert, in the course of his visit the morning following this compact with Mr. Lovaine cannot be thought extraordinary; because, however little interested might have been his own feelings, in ascertaining the degree of impression made by his ci-devant *protégé*, he was bound, in honour to his new ally, to relieve him with the utmost despatch from his present state of painful suspense.

" Did you find young Lovaine as agreeable as ever last night? I understood he was to spend the evening with you," inquired Mr. Benson, in a tone of assumed indifference.

Mrs. Lawlie had, however, learnt by this time, that a more agreeable theme could be found on which to dwell with Mr. Benson than the praises of young Lovaine, and she

therefore replied in the same tone of indifference, " Much as usual; he is certainly under
great obligations to you, for the pains you
have taken to improve his mind; but I sometimes fear that, although the good seed has
been sown in good soil, yet that the weeds
were not sufficiently exterminated at first, to
allow of its ever coming to perfection : the
produce will be, and is, greatly improved, but
the harvest will not be abundant."

There was a treacherous sparkle in the eyes
of Mr. Benson at the declaration of this opinion, that could not escape the observation of
a woman: for after all, though Mrs. Lawlie
did occasionally hold her sex in contempt, and
was, nominally, too great a philosopher to be a
coquette, still she was a woman—and more-

over possessed in an eminent degree that *finesse d'esprit*, that quick perception of character, which, it must be confessed, does more especially belong to the female half of human kind.

" I fear that your opinion is but too well-founded," he replied, though with an expression of countenance that spoke more of hope than of fear. Lovaine was born for better deeds than he will ever accomplish: he has been too long nursed in the lap of luxury—too long accustomed to the vices of the rich and idle—not to require the one, and not to look with indifference, if not with indulgence, on the other. That all-directing principle of action, love of self, must teach him to view with pleasure and complacency those evils by which he benefits; he has too direct an interest in

the continuance of existing and long-established abuses, to wish sincerely for their reform.
The cultivation of his naturally intelligent
mind by the exercise of his reasoning faculties,
may give him a clearer perception of justice
and expediency, but his principles will never
be of sufficient power to regulate his conduct
according to that perception."

" Yes," replied Mrs. Lawlie, " the education
bestowed upon him by his uncle has doubtless
been of serious disadvantage to him; for though
he is by no means unconscious of that fact, yet
so strong with him is the force of habit and
early prejudice, that I believe he is still much
attached to the said uncle, if not occasionally
influenced by him."

A pause ensued—and Mr. Benson's countenance bore stronger evidences of agitation than quite became the man of reason. Mrs. Lawlie also felt embarrassed. The conversation had gone on with great apparent fluency as yet; but there was something in this silence which seemed rather to portend a change in the nature, than a discontinuance of the subject: for their discourse had neither come to a natural close, nor had its course been turned by the starting of any fresh topic. Perhaps the recollection of Herbert's manner on the preceding evening had its share, both in suggesting the possibility of the conversation changing in its object, though not in its subject, and of some inquietude at that change.

That Mrs. Lawlie's presentiments were no false prophets, was proved in the first sen tence by which Mr. Benson broke the awful stillness that had reigned in the apartment for two or three minutes : a space of time scarcely noted in the ordinary occupations of life, but which appears little short of as many hours, when the mind is busily employed in speculating upon that which is to follow.

" Excuse," said he, " the liberty, if such you consider it, of what I am about to say. There can, I hope, be no doubt in your mind of the friendship and interest which I have long felt for the only woman whom I ever knew to be sufficiently above the weaknesses of her sex to be a rational and useful member of society." (Nothing flattered Mrs. Lawlie so much as being so considered; but at this moment she almost overlooked the compliment, in her anxiety to hear the conclusion of her friend's harangue.) " The opinion which you have just expressed of young Lovaine's character and abilities has satisfied my mind upon one point; I had feared that he was becoming, if not already become, an object of sufficient interest in your eyes, to blind you to those faults and imperfections, which, however much we may regret, truth compels, or at least ought to compel us to own, and from which justice requires that we withhold the admiration and confidence which are due to more real talent and exalted worth.

" I find, however, that I wronged you in so thinking, and you must forgive me. Of the state of his feelings I need not ask you—on that subject there is no doubt. I ask you not whether he has or has not actually obtruded their declaration· upon your ears; but let me entreat you, my dearest Mrs. Lawlie," (and here the philosopher drew his chair nearer to the fair subject of his sage advice; and, though of course unthinkingly, and merely from that inattention to his movements so naturally produced by the absorbing interest of his discourse, he laid his hand upon her's) " to be upon your guard with that young man. He is perhaps unconscious of that superiority of mind and acquirement which so endears you to those, whose habits and pursuits in life lead them to look for pleasure only in intellectual enjoyment—but he is not insensible to those graces of person, which' constitute in the society to which he has all his life belonged a woman's greatest—nay, her only charm."

(Mrs. Lawlie never knew before that Mr. Benson had ever perceived those personal attractions to which he had just alluded. Whether this discovery was likely to be offensive or agreeable to any woman, even to one of Mrs. Lawlie's truly intellectual pursuits, we leave to the decision of our female readers.)

" To mislead—to betray—and to abandon those whom they can deceive, is the boast of the class in which he was brought up; and although the partial reform, which myself and others have effected in his own principles, may induce him to admit the flagrancy of such despicable conduct, so long as he is free from the temptation to follow that example, yet I much fear that with the temptation would quickly appear the cloven foot. He is too much of an aristocrat at heart not to expect, as a right, the possession of whatever he covets. Teach him, then, that his wishes must be tempered by reason, and that rank, fashion, and wealth, sink into merited insignificance, when urged against the superior force of knowledge and reflection."

" Surely," replied Mrs. Lawlie, who at last took courage to interrupt this more salutary than agreeable advice, " you are rather hasty in your judgment; you can have no reason to assert thus positively the existence of those feelings towards myself, which you attribute to Mr. Lovaine."

" Pardon me; in that you are mistaken; as indeed I think you will allow, when I tell you that of those feelings, of which you are

disposed to doubt the existence, I was yester-
day morning informed by an individual to
whom you are unknown, and who could have
had no other means of obtaining information
upon the subject, but through Lovaine himself."

" Whom do you mean?" she eagerly inquired.

" His name I am not at liberty to mention.
He is as perfectly unknown to you, as you are
to him, and one whose feelings and opinions
are as wholly opposite to those which you
have hitherto maintained, as the extremes of
liberality and illiberality must ever be."

" But what proof have you that it was by
Mr. Lovaine that my name was mentioned to
this anonymous individual?" demanded Mrs.

Lawlie, half pleased at the supposed avowal of Herbert's preference for her, and yet half alarmed at its confession having come to the knowledge of Mr. Benson.

" Every proof but one," he replied, " and that was—excuse my openness—the want of respect with which my informer spoke of the individual concerning whom he had been selected as confidant. Of that diligent employment of your time, and judicious cultivation of your mind, which has gained you the applause of every thinking person, he spoke slightingly, if not with ridicule."

This was a sad downfall to Mrs. Lawlie's pride! The idea that Herbert could have spoken of her in such a manner as to have excited the ridicule of any one, mortified her

vanity, and aroused her anger. Forgetting at
the moment every other feeling, she was disposed at once to shut her doors for ever
against the youth whom she had hitherto
received with open arms, and who had certainly had no reason to think on the preceding
evening that his society was, in any way,
offensive to her.

Mr. Benson did not, however, approve of
such sudden and decisive measures; he knew
that they could not be adopted, without the
risk of some explanation of their cause being
demanded by Herbert. Perhaps the idea that
there is nothing so dangerous as an explanation, where the tender feelings are awakened
in one or both of the parties concerned — that
it gives an opportunity of talking of them-

selves, and of each other, which by acknow-
ledging, often strengthens those feelings, did
not occur to Mr. Benson, because he was pro-
fessedly ignorant upon such matters; but that
the part which he had taken in the affair
might come to young Lovaine's ears, should
Mrs. Lawlie be explicit as to the cause of her
change of conduct towards him, and that that
would be far from agreeable, did decidedly
occur to him. He did not, therefore, leave
her till she had promised him faithfully that
she would not make any sudden or violent
alteration in her manner towards Herbert,
although she would gradually diminish the
invitations which she had hitherto so kindly
offered him to her house.

Nor was this all, for, piqued beyond measure

at the idea of being the butt, instead of the idol of the man in whose favour she had, with so much liberality and candour, put by her well-founded dislike to the class to which he belonged, she willingly consented to keep Mr. Benson *au courant* of all particulars of their future interviews; hoping, by thus confiding in one who was well acquainted with his character, and her own real friend, she might not only preserve herself from the ignominious position of being the dupe of a mere man of fashion, but that in time, assisted by his counsels, she might so turn the tables upon Lovaine, the very first opportunity, as to afford a most brilliant illustration of " the biter bit !"

CHAPTER VIII.

Nothing could have been more agreeably successful to Mr. Benson than his visit to Mrs. Lawlie; and of course, no time was lost in communicating its result, according to agreement, to Mr. Lovaine.

That Herbert was the decided admirer of Mrs. Lawlie, Mr. Benson was more than ever convinced since his interview with that lady; but he was now also satisfied that there existed no reciprocity of sentiment. To have joined in Mr. Lovaine's prejudiced abuse of Mrs. Lawlie, would have been but very little con-

genial to his feelings; and by this timely discovery of her indifference towards Herbert, he
was not only spared the performance himself
of any such disagreeable part, in his future
conversations with Mr. Lovaine on the subject,
but was also enabled to moderate the vehemence of his dislike to that lady, without
diminishing his suspicious watchfulness of his
nephew.

Mr. Benson had, moreover, so adroitly con-
verted Mrs. Lawlie's indifference towards Herbert into anger, and her reserve into confidence
towards himself, that he was no longer in fear
that her judgment would be blinded, or her
time wasted, by the growing influence of a
young man, incapable of appreciating her real
merits.

Although Mr. Lovaine had promised that
he would make no allusion to his suspicions
respecting Mrs. Lawlie to Herbert, till Mr.
Benson thought it fit that he should do so, yet
his character was far from being one of sufficient
circumspection entirely to conceal his feelings
upon any subject that was uppermost in his
mind. It is true that he made no direct attack
upon his nephew; but no opportunity was lost
of taunting and twitting him about his manner
of passing his time; of his being obliged to
read in the morning, in order to be well received by the Blues in the evening—of the sin of
equivocation being greater than that of lying—
of the ingratitude of a want of confidence to
those who had a right to expect it, &c. &c.;
the precise meaning of which, Herbert was

often at a loss to comprehend. That these observations, however, were intended as so many
coups de pattes to him, he was left in no doubt
by the tone in which they were uttered; and
that a youth who was convinced upon reason
and principle, that he had long since attained
the age beyond which one man had no right
to control the actions of another, should be
irritated by such observations, cannot be
thought unnatural: besides, he was, in his opinion, the appointed, though unpaid champion
of justice; and to hear without reply, injustice
done to so warm an advocate of all that was
just and liberal as Mrs. Lawlie, would, therefore, have been a cowardly shrinking from
his duty; consequently he was at once following his inclination, and acting according to

his duty, in seldom failing to answer his uncle in such a manner as to increase the disapprobation with which that gentleman already regarded himself, his conduct, and his friends.

There is no state more unfortunate for the peace and union of relations and friends than that of ill disguised, but unavowed displeasure; it affords no opportunity for mutual justification and consequent reconciliation, and by causing a constant repetition of trifling offences, the extent of which is often unknown to him who commits them, a soreness is created between the parties, upon which the first wound that is inflicted, however slight, will quickly inflame to a dangerous, if not incurable degree.

The more Mr. Lovaine thought fit do decry his pursuits, or to speak dispaiagingly of the

advantages of female education, the more did
Herbert declare himself devoted to study, and
the more was his table strewed with pam-
phlets on radical reform, and also with the
more zest did he seek the society of her
whom he considered to have most benefited
by the pains she had bestowed upon her education.

Of his manner, and in fact of all that passed
during those visits, a faithful report was made
by Mrs. Lawlie to Mr. Benson; and by him
again were they detailed (though often revised
and corrected) to Mr. Lovaine; nor did it a
little increase his anger at the frequency of
Herbert's visits to Russell Square, when he was
convinced, that so far from being a victim to
the ingenious arts of a clever, designing wo-

man, he was, in fact, no better than an unprincipled, though hitherto unsuccessful, dis-
turber of conjugal felicity.

It was in this unpleasant and unharmonious
state of feeling that Herbert and his uncle remained for some time. Both kept up their intercourse with Mr. Benson; Herbert, because
he still considered him as the man of the
greatest talent he had ever known, and because he considered himself to be under deep
and lasting obligations to him, for having with-
drawn him from all his former occupations
and society; and his uncle, because it was
through him that he obtained the information
which he was so desirous of possessing, and
because, as he believed him to entertain the
same opinions as himself on all those subjects

on which Mr. Benson had had the good taste not to contradict him, he regarded him as a man of good sense and sound judgment.

As, however, Mr. Benson never failed to impress upon Mr. Lovaine the necessity of the non-mention of his name in that affair which had become their particular *point de réunion*, Herbert was quite ignorant of the extent of their intimacy; though that they should not have entertained at first sight too profound a contempt for each other ever to meet again, did always seem most surprising to him; and was only accounted for by the consideration, that a man of Mr. Benson's abilities commanded respect, even from those who were most opposed to him in character and opinions. He knew that they occasionally met; indeed,

Mr. Benson had once or twice accompanied him to Mr. Lovaine's residence; but, as we have said before, he had no idea of the terms on which they were together. Had he been so, he would perhaps have applied to Mr. Benson to solve the meaning of many a pointed remark made by his uncle, the sting of which he invariably felt inclined to resent, because he knew it was meant to be piercing, though he knew not how.

To Mr. Benson, however, no hint of these little tiffs was ever breathed by Herbert, and invariably did they reach his ears through Mr. Lovaine; consequently, Herbert had invariably the appearance of being in the wrong, and Mr. Benson did but give his opinion conscientiously when he said that he thought so.

Herbert abstained from all mention of his disagreements with his uncle, from the double reason of not wishing to obtrude family matters upon a third, and, as he thought, uninterested person; and from not caring to have known by any one the extent to which his uncle still thought proper to carry his interference, and interpose his authority. But to Mr. Benson, the feeling that he was treated with less confidence by his disciple (over whom he had never before doubted his entire influence) than he considered his due, did not dispose him to look with a very favourable eye upon his conduct; and whilst busily employed in gaining considerable ascendancy over the elder Mr. Lovaine, he was growing more and more dissatisfied with the younger, who was so blind to his own interests as not to apply to him for advice.

Mrs. Lawlie had been guilty of no such dereliction of duty; for if she had not actually sought his advice, she had paid him the still higher compliment of following it, so far as regarded her conduct towards Herbert; for as Mr. Benson had advised her not to make any sudden or marked change, she saw no reason against his being invited to dinner to meet Mrs. Lovechild, and a few more, upon whom he had made, in spite of his disadvantageous birth and education, a very favourable impression: for though Mrs. Lawlie's distrust of Herbert had been too strongly awakened not secure her from all danger of bestowing too great a portion of her own regard upon him, yet to have appeared entirely to cast him off, or, as some ill-natured, misjudging people would have said, to lose the patronage of him, would have been useless and unkind. To dinner, therefore, he was invited; and the invitation was accepted with the greater pleasure, as an interval of unusual length had elapsed since the last time of that honour having been conferred upon him.

Herbert had returned to his lodgings early in the afternoon, for the purpose of reading, or perhaps (as his uncle sometimes imputed to him) for the purpose of shining with unusual brilliancy at Mrs. Lawlie's Upon entering the room, he found two letters lying on his table, one from his cousin, the other from his aunt. They had both been written subsequent

to the departure of the De Cliffords, and previous to the proposal of Lord Goldsborough.

The contents of Elinor's letter were principally regrets at the departure of her friends,
and rapturous commendations of Emily's perfections. The letter from his aunt also contained regrets at the breaking up of so pleasant
a party, and some encomiums upon Emily,
who, she observed, was well calculated to make
the happiness of whomever she married; and,
indeed, in proof of how highly she was in Mrs.
Lovaine's good graces, she wound up her little
chapter upon her, by expressing her sincere
hope that the intelligence which she had just
heard from Mrs. —— was true, *viz.* that she
was likely to marry Mr. Gordon, the eldest
son of Lord Melrose, who would have Glen-

carry Castle, in Scotland, besides a good
landed estate in the north of England; indeed, upon whom all the property was en-
tailed, and against whom, she believed, there
was nothing to be said; he was going, as she
had been informed, to meet the De Cliffords
at Brussels, for the express purpose of pro-
posing to Emily, and that the marriage would
take place immediately on their arrival in
England.

Herbert could hardly conceal from himself,
as he read the letter, how little he entered into
the good wishes of his aunt, for the comfortable establishment of Miss De Clifford; he
threw it down, and inwardly vituperated the
detestable system of marrying girls to castles
and estates, instead of to men; he felt more

convinced than he had ever been before, of the
propriety of the equal division of property,
because it was more calculated to prevent the
present practice of mothers bringing their
daughters to market. He owned that the
premium upon that practice was now too high;
that the choice was often between beggary and
magnificence, poverty and luxury. The temptation was certainly great; and naturally,
therefore, much too great to be resisted by the
parents of children, whose habits and education had taught them to view with greater
reverence and admiration the aristocracy of
birth and wealth, than the distinctions of merit
and talent.

These reflections were for a moment interrupted by the discovery of a few lines on the

back of his aunt's letter, written subsequently
to the rest, and which had, on the first reading,
escaped his observation. They were as follows:—" The event, of which I have given
your uncle full particulars, took place after I
had closed this letter; and I now only open it
to beg you will lose no time in going to him
after the receipt of it, in case you are not with
him when it arrives. I hope, however, that
you will not be together, for I have directed
the letters to your respective residences, on
purpose to oblige you to guess the good news
which he has to tell you. You will, I am sure,
be as much delighted as any of us."

" What childish nonsense !" muttered Herbert half aloud, " to be made to guess. Why
the deuce could not my aunt have told me at

once what she had to say, if it was worth telling at all !"

He did, however, for a few minutes, apply his mind to guess; and his first surmise was that she had heard of the actual celebration of Miss De Clifford's marriage. Upon reflection, however, he rejected the idea of her being concerned in the matter, as improbable in the extreme; though the circumstance of its having crossed his mind appeared to have by no means added to the serenity of his temper.

Having settled that it was only some frivolous nonsense, of which he would not ask an explanation from his uncle when he returned from dinner, he was beginning to muse again upon the first part of the letter, whilst he mechanically reached down the books which he had come home for the purpose of perusing, when, with a countenance full of importance, not unmixed with satisfaction, entered Mr. Lovaine.

" Well, Herbert! have you guessed the news from Spa? Your aunt tells me she was going to put your powers of divination to the test: so I am come to see whether you have been clever enough to solve the riddle, or to put you out of your pain, if you are still racking your brain to make it out."

Herbert well remembered that it had ever been a favourite custom, both with his uncle and aunt, when he was a little boy, and that any good fortune, such as a child's ball, or a party to Astley's, or a game at snap-dragon, or a plum-cake, awaited him, to exercise his ingenuity in making him guess what was going to happen; consequently, he was not particularly pleased at the form in which this piece of intelligence, whatever it might be, was to be communicated to him: it struck him as being puerile and ridiculous; and with a perverseness of feeling more common than praiseworthy in mankind, he determined to treat with indifference that which was made of so much importance by others.

" Really, Sir," he carelessly replied, " my aunt seems to have strangely reckoned upon a talent which I certainly do not possess for unravelling a mystery, or upon my being what is called a lucky guesser; but I fear, if my knowledge of this great and important event depended solely upon that, I should remain in ignorance to the end of my days."

Mr. Lovaine did not at all like this mode of answering; moreover, as he had been in good spirits, and in good-humour, when he entered the room, he was not pleased at seeing Herbert's grave face, or at hearing his not very good-humoured reply. He always liked sympathy; he liked people to be gay or sad, warm or cold, good or ill-humoured, according as he felt himself; and if he had not at this moment been much too full of the event of his daughter's marriage, (and that this was the intelligence which he had just received, our readers have no doubt guessed, though Herbert had not,) to refrain from talking to some one upon the subject, he would immediately have left the house in dudgeon; but wishing to discuss the matter with one whose affection and interest for Elinor he did not, and could not doubt, he abstained from any such measure, though, perhaps, he did not entirely preserve his good humour.

" Your studies don't seem to have sharpened your wits, young man, as much as might have been expected. I swear I think you were a quicker lad before you took to reading than you have been since; however, do you give up the point? and must I tell you the news, by reading to you the letter I have received from your aunt?"

"I shall be very happy," replied Herbert, in

the same tone of indifference in which he had
spoken before, " to hear my aunt's letter;
though, as I am not particularly curious, I
dare say it would be no great affliction to me
not to hear this important bit of intelligence."

" I did not expect this unkind indifference,
Herbert, from you, where Elinor was concerned," retorted Mr. Lovaine, who began to
consider his child as much aggrieved by the
insouciance of Herbert, as if he had really
known that there was any thing to be heard
respecting her.

" I think, Sir, the unkindness consists rather in withholding from me any circumstance
relating to one whom I have ever loved as a

sister," said Herbert, whose interest and curiosity were at once aroused when his cousin's name was mentioned.

" Well, well! I see you will never make it all out, unless I help you to the first part of the story ; so I will tell you at once, that Elinor is going to be married—and to whom, do you think ?"

Herbert's surprise was so great, that he was on the point of forgetting his previous state of irritation; perhaps too, the person whom it occurred to him to name, though certainly from no other reason than that the individual was, at that moment, uppermost in his thoughts, contributed in some degree to dispel the gloom which had hung on his brow from the time he had perused his own letters from Spa.

" Elinor going to be married!" he ex-claimed. " Is it to Mr. Gordon? For God's sake, Sir, tell me to whom?"

" Psha! psha! why Mr. Gordon is to mar-ry Elinor's friend, not herself. What are you thinking about? Try once more."

It was, however, too late to tell him to think again. All the irritation under which he was labouring when his uncle had first entered the room, had returned upon him now tenfold; and had not the impatience which Mr. Lovaine felt to tell his news far exceeded the quickness evinced by Herbert in guessing, he would certainly have been left in as complete a state of ignorance when they separated, as he was when they met.

His exclamation, upon being informed that

Lord Goldsborough was the person destined to be Mr. Lovaine's son-in-law, of, "Is it possible that she is to be so sacrificed?" was in no small degree offensive to that gentleman. Nothing could, in fact, be more opposite than their impression of Lord Goldsborough, or their views upon the subject.

Lord Reading was what is usually termed a very worthy excellent man, a regular church and state nobleman, who hated innovations of all sorts to Mr. Lovaine's heart's content, and was therefore, in his opinion, a very safe politician—of a very old family, and very large property. They had been slightly acquainted for a great many years—they had always agreed on whatever subjects they had discussed; consequently, Lord Reading held a

very high place in the good graces of Mr. Lovaine—and that the son, whom he had never
seen, should be the *fac-simile* of his father, and
therefore worthy of his dear Elinor, he did
not for a moment doubt.

It must be allowed, that the glowing de-
scriptions of Mrs. Lovaine, not only of his
Lordship's perfections, but also of his devotion to their daughter, greatly tended to
heighten and justify this prejudice; although
we shrewdly suspect that it would have been
entertained, had there not been such reasonable
grounds for its existence ; the jump from Mr.
Lovaine's premises to his conclusions being,
in general, somewhat remarkable for its rapidity.

Herbert had no personal knowledge of Lord

Reading, but had been at college with Lord Goldsborough; and so long as they had continued to meet in society afterwards, they had kept up the acquaintance which they had there made, though rather because it is difficult, if not impossible, for people to drop each other (when constantly meeting) without a quarrel, or other ostensible pretext, than because they took the least pleasure in the company of each other,

In the days of Herbert's gaiety and high spirits, he had, in common with friends who were gay and open-hearted as himself, ridiculed Lord Goldsborough for being pompous; called him "The polished Heir-apparent," " the priggish young Nobleman," "the Representative of Orthodoxy," &c. &c. &c.; had more than once persuaded him to cut a young lady, (who could scarcely tolerate him) for making *a set* at him.   Lord Goldsborough had, in short, been more or less the butt of the little knot of young men, who, from having been his cotemporaries at Christ Church, well knew what were his foibles, and how to make them appear in the most ridiculous point of view.

When, however, Herbert became studious, grave, and reserved, *i. e.* what he considered to be literary and political, or what his uncle would have called pedantic and radical, Lord Goldsborough had been to his mind one of the most striking instances of the bad effects of the present system of things in general. The idea, that such a man as Lord Goldsborough would have an hereditary voice in the

legislature of his country, besides the power of
returning more than one nominal representative of the people, was always to him a convincing proof of the unsoundness of our government, and of the fallacy of the boasted
wisdom of our ancestors. Lord Goldsborough
was, in fact, it must be confessed, a most
excellent specimen of the evils likely to accrue
from the situation to which he was born, and
the education which he had received; and
whenever Herbert most trembled for the safety and welfare of his country, it was when he
pictured to himself the possibility of its counsels being directed by Lord Goldsborough, or
his *semblables.*

With such feelings towards the young nobleman in question, it was very natural that

Herbert should feel far from pleased or satisfied at hearing that to *him* his cousin was to be
united. For her, he had not only a great affection, but he had also formed a little plan of
endeavouring, on her return home, to lead
her mind to the consideration of such subjects
as Mrs. Lawlie so successfully handled. He
had, moreover, been very often provoked at
the love of fashion, which his aunt had been
but at small pains to conceal in her letters;
and he felt sure that Elinor had been forced
into the acceptance of a man whom she must
despise, and he was indignant at the manner
in which she had thus been sacrificed.

"Sacrificed! why, what the devil do you
mean?" was Mr. Lovaine's first exclamation
and interrogatory, after Herbert's expression

of this opinion; and before he had time to explain his meaning, his indignation was considerably increased by the unmerited encomiums that were passed upon his Lordship by Mr. Lovaine. Herbert utterly denied the truth of his uncle's assertions, and in terms which shewed that his temper or his principles had produced considerable oblivion in his mind, both of their relative positions and of their respective ages.

Whilst thus engaged in angry altercation, the servant entered and informed Herbert that Mrs. Lawlie had just sent to acquaint him that she dined an hour later than usual, and hoped it would not be inconvenient to him.

Nothing could be more inopportune, at that

moment, than such a reminder of Mrs. Lawlie's
name and existence; it lent fresh vigour to
Mr. Lovaine's increasing ire. His promise to
Mr. Benson was so far remembered, that no
mention whatever was made of that gentleman,
but of his further promise to await Mr. Benson's advice respecting the time and the manner in which he should broach the subject to
his nephew, all recollection was gone. Lord
Goldsborough, the original cause of their dispute, was for the time forgotten. Mr. Lovaine openly accused Herbert of equivocation,
deception, and ingratitude towards himself;
taxed him with evil designs against the honour
of the woman whom he pretended to admire
and respect; and finally asserted his own au-

thoritative right to forbid the frequency, if not altogether the continuance of his visits to Russell Square.

Herbert's temper and feelings were now irritated beyond all control. He scorned to repel the accusations of his uncle; but in the most explicit and unmeasured terms denied his right of interference, and boldly asserted his own independence, and his determination to be in future the sole arbiter of his own thoughts, words, and deeds.

With every reply the anger of each was increased, till Mr. Lovaine snatching up his hat, and declaring that he would no longer bear to be insulted where he ought to be respected, hastily quitted the house.

That his uncle had thus abruptly departed

in anger, Herbert did not scruple to acknowledge to himself that he regretted; but that he
had done nothing more than his duty to himself, in adopting the line of conduct which had
produced that anger; he had no doubt; therefore with his regret no self-reproach was
mingled.

That his nephew had proved himself unworthy of his affection, Mr. Lovaine did not
hesitate to acknowledge was a circumstance
that gave him real pain; but that he had done
only his duty in reproving him so severely,
and in assuming so much authority over him,
he entertained no doubt: therefore with his
regrets also was mingled no self-reproach; and
in this state of feelings, it would be difficult
to say which of the two was the most likely, or

rather unlikely, to make the first advance towards a reconciliation. They had often indulged in the petty warfare of squabbling and bickering, but this was their first decided quarrel.

It is a very dangerous thing for those who are bound by the ties of blood or matrimony, ever to discover the possibility of coming to an open rupture. How seldom does it happen, in such cases, that the first quarrel stands alone, or unsucceeded by similar discords!

CHAPTER IX.

ALTHOUGH, as we have before stated, neither Mr. Lovaine or Herbert allowed themselves to be tormented by the pangs of self-reproach, yet to say with truth that either was comfortable, under the existing circum-stances, would be impossible. They each felt it out of the question, though from different motives, to seek the other. Herbert knew that such a step would be construed by his uncle into an acknowledgment of error, and a proof of repentance. Mr. Lovaine, on the other hand, was equally afraid that any such measure on his part, would be considered as a recognition of the independence assumed by Herbert, and would form a dangerous precedent in case of future disagreement.

It so happened that at the time of this most unpleasant interview Mr. Benson was out of town, attending upon the death of a relation: for though it must in justice be said that he never alluded to such beings, yet still he had relations in the world; and from the one whose eyes he had just closed, and of whose funeral he was waiting to assist, he inherited a small sum of money, the produce of the industrious, if not always respectable labour of an attorney.

On his return, his first care was to seek Mrs. Lawlie; not however finding her at home, he bent his steps to the other end of the town, and sought, with more success, Mr. Lovaine. Mr. Benson inquired, in the course of his visit, whether he had seen Herbert on that day; and it did not escape his observation, that Mr. Lovaine's manner was somewhat embarrassed at the question, and that he very quickly turned the conversation to another subject.

. Mr. Benson was at a loss to comprehend this change; but as he perceived no diminution of cordiality in Mr. Lovaine's manner towards him, he was satisfied that he continued in his usual high favour with that gentleman, and he had sufficient tact never to press the discussion of any topic which did not seem to be a welcome one at the moment.

Mr. Lovaine was extremely pleased at this

instance of proper discretion in Mr. Benson, because it spared him the awkward task of confessing his own inconsistency, in having acted directly contrary to all his professions of being guided, in his conduct towards his nephew, entirely by the advice of Mr. Benson.

The mystery of this embarrassment was however in some degree unravelled the following morning, when Mr. Benson made another and more successful call upon Mrs. Lawlie. In answer to his usual interrogations respecting Herbert's visits, he found that during his absence they had been both longer and more frequent than before: moreover, he was not quite pleased with the tone in which she spoke of young Lovaine: he began to fear that she was in danger of forgetting the resentment which he had stirred within her against him. She spoke of his having been in low spirits with more compassion than was entirely agreeable to him.

Mrs. Lawlie attributed his occasional dejection to a quarrel which she understood to have taken place between him and his prejudiced illiberal uncle; of the cause of which she was ignorant, but for which she seemed disposed rather to blame the elder than the younger Lovaine. She owned that he had confided to her the existence of the quarrel, and had implied that it had arisen from the very different opinions which they each entertained of the character of the man who was destined to marry his cousin; but to what this had afterwards led, he had so positively declined informing her, that she, with truth, declared herself to be in perfect ignorance upon the subject.

The idea that Mrs. Lawlie herself had formed part of their ground of dispute, which would at once account both for the reserve in Herbert, and for the embarrassment of Mr. Lovaine, when he inquired after his nephew, instantly occurred to Mr. Benson's mind, and he determined to lose no time in making himself master of the whole of that which Mrs. Lawlie knew but in part.

It was his intention to have derived his information from Mr. Lovaine; but before he again saw him, he had learnt from Herbert himself quite enough to determine upon his own line of conduct. They had accidentally met in the street—neither had any engagement—and they agreed to dine and spend the evening together.

Herbert was not naturally reserved; or at least he was (like most other people) never very reserved, when he not only thought himself in the right, but made sure of being considered equally so by the person to whom he opened his mind. He therefore did not conceal from Mr. Benson the terms on which he then was with his uncle, and the necessity under which he felt himself to assert his own independence, in order to escape from the positive thraldom in which his uncle attempted to keep him.

When speaking of Mr. Lovaine's inter-

ference with respect to Mrs. Lawlie, he said,
" I could not bear to be treated like a child
of ten years old, and I wished him to know it.
Whatever may be my feelings towards Mrs.
Lawlie, I certainly have arrived at an age
when I may be considered the fairest and best
judge of what concerns myself. Had my uncle
offered me his advice as my equal, I might
have been disposed to listen, and perhaps, if
possible, to follow it; but I cannot submit to
be domineered over, as if *junior* and *inferior*
were synonymous—but as it is, if it were even
contrary to my inclination so to do, I would
rather double the length and frequency of my
visits to Russell Square, than allow him to
imagine that I am still to be lectured, or

ordered, or bullied into obedience to his commands."

Mr. Benson was almost tempted to thank him for this hint. The warmth with which he spoke convinced him he was in earnest, and he had no particular wish for him to adopt such a measure as the one he had just proposed, in order to convince his uncle that he was come to years of discretion. He therefore instantly saw that a speedy reconciliation between them was the most desirable measure to effect.

That Herbert's feelings could be worked upon by kindness, Mr. Benson suspected; that his reason was open to conviction he knew; and that neither his high spirit or temper would brook control, he was now entirely persuaded; and he determined to act accordingly. He only waited therefore for the first favourable opportunity to perform the amiable part of peace-maker between Mr. Lovaine and Herbert.

This opportunity soon offered; and Mr. Benson wisely adopted the best means of gaining and increasing towards himself the attentions and good-will of Mr. Lovaine, by the manner in which he introduced the subject to him, instead of putting him under the disagreeable necessity of detailing himself all that had passed relative to the quarrel. He with some ingenuity contrived, not only to shew his acquaintance with the circumstance, but to interest Mr. Lovaine, by reporting the manner in which Mrs. Lawlie had in vain endeavoured to extract from Herbert the cause of this unfortunate disagreement.

But so desirable an object as a reconciliation, or- at least so complete a reconciliation as was likely to increase the power and influence of Mr. Lovaine over the indignant and independent feelings of his nephew, and which would alone serve the present purpose of Mr. Benson, was not to be effected without much difficulty from both parties. He had however in an eminent degree the gift of perseverance, and he did not now exercise it in vain: for after much dexterous management of each, much palliation of all that had been said of and to each other, after perhaps even an occasional little forgery of some conciliatory observations, that might have been, but never were made, by one party or the other, his endeavours were crowned with success.

As, however, this laudable enterprize had not been undertaken by Mr. Benson wholly and solely from the love of harmony and union, but from the additional motive of having his own particular interest to assist by the performance of so praiseworthy a part as that of peace-maker, he naturally turned his thoughts to the consideration of the manner in which he could best continue to further the end which he had in view.

It was clear that Herbert would not only be uninfluenced by the assumption of authority in his uncle, but that he would no longer brook restraint, or be obedient to command. It was not, however, so clear that, though he might rebel at what he considered tyranny and oppression, he might not be touched by the voice of kindness; that he might not be won into compliance with wishes expressed with gentleness, or yield to advice, when given as a friend and equal, not as a preceptor and superior.

To impress Mr. Lovaine with the policy of adopting such a line of conduct towards his nephew was no easy task. Mr. Benson's influence was, however, rapidly becoming all-powerful in that quarter; and if he did not succeed in opening the eyes of Mr. Lovaine to all the wisdom and incontrovertibility of his arguments, he had the gratification of receiving a still higher tribute to his judgment and sagacity in general, by the power allowed him of leading blindfold one who prided himself, above all other things, in never being led.

After the reconciliation between Mr. Lovaine and Herbert, the name of Mrs. Lawlie, by the recommendation of Mr. Benson, was at first never mentioned. She was afterwards casually named, in the course of conversation, as if to show that neither had retained any unpleasant recollections of their late quarrel, till at last a greater degree of ease and good feeling appeared, and actually did exist between them, than had done for some time previous to the bursting of that storm which had so long been gathering.

Then was the moment for Mr. Benson to

recommend, with the best chance of success, the trial of the *soothing system.* Nor was the opportunity thrown away upon him: he actually dictated the manner, and almost the very words, to Mr. Lovaine, in which he was to address his nephew upon the subject. Herbert was much surprised at the tone his uncle adopted towards him, but was doubly pleased with him, and gratified at the change, because he considered it as the result of his own recent spirited resistance of the undue exercise of authority.

Mr. Benson perceiving this, did not fail to encourage Herbert in the idea; at the same time remarking, that having once established his independence, it would be wiser to continue the good understanding which now existed be-

tween them, by abstaining from all unnecessary disagreements, than to constantly remind
his uncle of the emancipation he had effected,
by refusing to listen to his advice and opinions,
when offered upon any subject, merely because they were his.

Herbert was sufficiently impressed with the
good sense of this remark, and sufficiently
satisfied, both with himself and Mr. Lovaine,
to act upon it in a manner which not only
pleased his uncle, but persuaded both, more
than ever, of the wisdom of Mr. Benson.   Not
a syllable of abuse of Mrs. Lawlie was ever
breathed by Mr. Lovaine, lest it should arouse
Herbert's spirit; no sneers or taunts were ever
thrown out upon the acquisition of learning,
either in man or woman.   Every thing, in

short, that had tended to irritate each other's feelings previous to their quarrel, was now carefully avoided, *de part et d'autre;* but fears were very gently expressed by Mr. Lovaine, that the too frequent repetition of Herbert's visits to Mrs. Lawlie might, however unjustly, cast a suspicion upon her. Hints were occasionally thrown out, that it became the part of an honourable man to forego his own pleasure, sooner than, even in appearance, to compromise the honour and reputation of a woman; till at last, won by the kindness of his uncle's manner, and really fearful lest he should endanger the reputation of one for whom he felt so high a respect (for that he implicitly believed her to be all that she herself aspired to make him and others believe of her, was most strictly true), the frequency of his visits began to diminish.

Upon this change Mr. Benson did not fail to make Mrs. Lawlie put a no very favourable construction; and ere long, Herbert became sensible of sufficient difference in the warmth with which he was received in Russell Square, to no longer make his compliance with his uncle's wishes as much at variance-with his own feelings as he had at first imagined. Mr. Benson, in fact, completely succeeded in ridding himself of the presence of Herbert, where he had feared him as a competitor; and, for that purpose, he had done the good deed of restoring at. least temporary peace and harmony between divided relations.

This great work had, however, been achieved

only by the constant exercise of the powerful influence of Mr. Benson in imposing silence to each, upon all those subjects which had proved never-failing sources of disagreement. Had they been touched upon, it is not to be supposed that Mr. Lovaine, could have been so suddenly altered in disposition as to have controlled his temper; or Herbert in principle as to have concealed his spirit of rebellion. How, far, therefore, the good footing on which they now stood was likely to remain, when Mr. Benson no longer thought it necessary to his own ends to lend his aid to its support, we trust our readers will have the patience to ascertain in the following chapter.

CHAPTER X.

THE time was now fast approaching when
Mr. Lovaine hoped to be once more cheered
by the presence of his wife and daughter.
With the latter, he was never otherwise than
pleased and satisfied; and he longed to fold
again to his heart his only child, the object of
his fondest affections. Nor did he look forward
with much less pleasure to the thoughts of
again beholding the chosen partner of his life.
Many a little difference, many a conjugal dispute, had been lulled by long absence into
oblivion. He had felt the loneliness of his

home when no longer graced by female society. Even Mrs. Lovaine's sin of going abroad, when she might have staid at home, had for some time lost much of its enormity in his opinion, in consequence of hearing that both she and Elinor lived chiefly with their own *compatriotes* on the Continent. But now that the result was Elinor's intended marriage with a young man of such family, fortune, and promise, as Lord Goldsborough, it was more than forgiven —it was sanctioned, it was almost applauded.

Herbert also looked forward with real pleasure to the prospect of the return of his aunt and ·cousin; but that circumstance which heightened the joy of his uncle, tinged his with melancholy: though, when acting under the immediate influence of Mr. Benson, he had abstained from any further expression of his opinion of Lord Goldsborough to Mr. Lovaine, yet it was, in fact, unchanged ; he disliked him so much that he could never divest himself of the impression that Elinor had not, in the case of her prospective marriage, been the unbiassed arbitress of her own fate.

" She cannot," thought he, " be so altered in taste and feeling, to say nothing of the reason and judgment which, at her age, one might hope she would have possessed, as to like, nay, to love and esteem, such a man as he to whom she is engaged !" And in this opinion he was the more confirmed by the cold and distant manner in which Elinor had herself alluded to her future prospects and affianced Lord.

Not one expression of happiness, not a single remark upon the character of Lord Goldsborough, had escaped her pen when writing to Herbert. He comforted himself, however, with the reflection that he would leave no stone unturned to discover her real sentiments upon the subject, as soon as she returned to England; and was equally determined, should his suspicions be well-founded, instantly to adopt some decisive measure to prevent what, under almost any circumstance, he considered to be an unwarrantable sacrifice of his cousin.

Poor Elinor! She was not fated to benefit by any such friendly interference. Previous to the reconciliation that took place between Herbert and his uncle, and at the time, there-

fore, when the feelings of the latter were most
irritated against the former, he had not disguised from Mrs. Lovaine both the cause and
the extent of his anger. He accurately detailed to her the opinions expressed by Herbert of the character of their future son-in-law,
his improper attachment to Mrs. Lawlie, and
his resolute defiance of his authority.

Mrs. Lovaine did not think proper to impart to Elinor the remarks which were made
by her cousin upon Lord Goldsborough, because she was sure it would be such an unnecessary trial of her feelings to hear a word,
even a syllable uttered, or of a thought entertained against the object of her tenderest affections. Whether Elinor would not, however,
have borne her cousin's remarks with more

patience and philosophy than did her mother, may at least be considered as doubtful.

Of the two other counts against Herbert, Mrs. Lovaine had no scruple in informing her daughter. The idea of a quarrel between two relations so near and dear to her as her father and her cousin, was one which Elinor had never contemplated as possible. She had yet to learn the influence of vanity and pride on the temper of mankind. She was young in her knowledge of the evil passions, for she had never in herself experienced their force. Her spirits had lost their usual tone, from the hour of her engagement to Lord Goldsborough; and although, from the repeated assurance of her mother that she was rather oppressed with joy than sorrow, and though she underwent no

self-examination as to the cause of this change,
yet she seemed but to wait for some ostensible
subject, of grief on which she might dwell,
something ·to ·justify the melancholy that depressed her.

·The account given by Mr. Lovaine of the
misconduct of Herbert gave at once a·name
and·an increase of cause for her sorrow. She
had never had courage to answer the letter she
had received from her friend Emily, the day
previous to the declaration of Lord Goldsborough. She had often and often sat down
with the intention of so doing; but she had
always found some excuse that made it impos-
sible·for her to write at that moment. She
told herself that she wished to write a·long
letter to Emily, and to tell her every thing that

had passed : but the detail gave her no pleasure
to write, and she therefore doubted the pleasure it would give to read ; for never do we so
much mistrust our powers of pleasing, as when
we are not pleased ourselves.

Mrs. Lovaine knew that Elinor had not
written, though she did not require to see all
the letters which her daughter wrote. She was
surprised at this want of *empressement* to communicate so important an event ; and having,
from the moment of Lord Goldsborough's proposal, herself almost forgotten the existence of
William De Clifford, she attributed her silence
solely to indolence, and therefore recommended strongly that she should no longer
delay answering Miss De Clifford's letter, and
announcing her own happiness, lest by being

anticipated in the news by some more active and less interested person, she should be re-proached for unkindness or want of con-fidence.

Elinor felt the truth of this remark, and with a heavy heart sat down to tell her friend how happy she was.   That she did not omit to mention her matrimonial prospects was most true; but she stated little more than the fact of Lord Goldsborough's proposal (which she owned had been to her wholly unexpected, though her mother declared that she had long perceived his attachment); her acceptance, and their intended marriage, so soon as Lord Golds-borough returned from Italy to England.

The remainder of the letter (and Elinor fulfilled her intention of making it a long one) consisted of details of her unhappiness, no less at the quarrel which had taken place between her father and Herbert, than that its cause should have been an unworthy attachment to such a woman as Mrs. Lawlie had been described by Mr. Lovaine, and a want of respect to his uncle.

Elinor was perfectly right in mistrusting the pleasure which Miss De Clifford would derive from the receipt of her letter; it was certainly not calculated to inspire more happiness on its perusal than had dictated its composition.

The indignation of Mrs. Lovaine had been somewhat aroused by hearing of the want of respect evinced by Herbert towards his uncle; but when she found that he had presumed to decry one so much his superior in rank, talent,

and acquirement, as Lord Goldsborough; a
man who, in her eyes at that moment, was the
representative of all earthly perfection, she
was furious; and the language which she
adopted, in her letters to her husband, was
far from conciliatory, and was but very little
calculated to diminish whatever wrath was
kindled in the bosom of Mr. Lovaine against
him.

Mrs. Lovaine was not naturally of a vin-
dictive or a malevolent disposition; but she
was too eager and anxious for the fulfilment of
her hopes respecting Elinor, not to adopt any
.steps that might avert the possibility of their
being frustrated; and though she knew that
Mr. Lovaine had actually quarrelled with Herbert, and that his having done so was partly in

consequence of the opinions he had expressed respecting Lord Goldsborough, yet she so dreaded the chance of his influencing his uncle against her idol, should they again be speedily reconciled, that her very nature seemed to change from fear.

Mrs. Lovaine might, however, have spared herself the unamiable office of increasing instead of diminishing the anger of her offended husband, for Herbert had more reason to dread than to be dreaded upon the occasion. His uncle's prejudices were too firm to be uprooted by a direct attack; he could be taken by stratagem, and was so taken by Mr. Benson; but an open assault was sure to be manfully and successfully resisted by him.

Mrs. Lovaine prevented Elinor writing to

Herbert, from the time of her hearing the
manner in which he had expressed himself
upon the subject of his cousin's marriage with
Lord Goldsborough, fearful lest he should in-
dulge in the repetition of any such expressions,
when writing to the promised bride of a man
that he so openly despised. Herbert construed this silence into a convincing proof of
poor Elinor's unhappiness at the step she had
been forced into taking, and her dread at the
still further and more desperate one which
was in store for her when she arrived in England; and he felt more and more determined,
each post-day that brought him no letter from
her, to be her champion, and to rescue her
from the trammels of this unfortunate engagement, so soon as her return home should

afford him the means of personal communication.

Mrs. Lovaine did not, however, think it necessary to place a similar restriction on herself to that which she had inflicted on her daughter, with respect to addressing Herbert in writing; and a somewhat angry correspondence, in which neither deemed it necessary to spare the feelings of the other, instantly commenced. Nor even when, acting under the rule and guidance of Mr. Benson, Herbert and his uncle were taught to be prudent and forbearing one to another, did this correspondence cease; for as it more regarded Herbert's feelings towards Lord Goldsborough than towards Mrs. Lawlie, Mr. Benson had not thought it worthy of his interference. He knew from

Mr. Lovaine that such a correspondence was maintained, and he took care that no vituperation contained in the letters of Mrs. Lovaine to her husband, upon the conduct of Herbert, should interrupt the plan. of operation which he had chalked out for that gentleman; but beyond that he had no interest in their family disputes, and therefore offered no advice upon the subject.

When not only the reconciliation, but its more-ultimate object, in Mr. Benson's eyes, the secession of Herbert from the house of Lawlie had been effected, he no longer thought himself bound to devote much of his time to the preservation of the peace which he had established. Indeed, from the period when Herbert ceased to frequent the drawing-room of ·

Mrs. Lawlie, he had felt himself so decidedly called upon to spend there the greater portion of his time, lest from that circumstance, as well as from the long absence of the money-getting Mr. Lawlie, she should feel the want of social intercourse, for which (although she rather despised the idea of wanting *company*, when so called) she had a considerable taste, that it was quite impossible for him to keep the same vigilant watch as formerly over the words and deeds—nay, almost over the very thoughts of two other individuals. It is true that he had no abstract wish that Herbert and his uncle should disagree, but as he had no longer any personal interest in their agreeing, he left them to act according to their own discretion; a quality with which

neither were highly gifted, and of which, unfortunately, the disposition of each required a
most frequent exercise, *vis-à-vis* of each
other.

Mr. Benson would always account, to the
satisfaction of Mr. Lovaine, and the admiration
of Herbert, for any diminution in the usual
frequency of his visits, by pleading to the
former the excuse of increase of professional
business, and to the latter that of an intention speedily to publish, in the form of a
pamphlet, his ideas upon " Government,"
" Parliamentary Reform," " Public Education," or some such important matter; and
though the said pamphlet did not appear when
Herbert was anxiously expecting it to do so,
yet Mr. Benson's reasons for the delay were

far too plausible for him to doubt their truth, and still less to imagine that his time had been so much otherwise engrossed, that in point of fact not one word of the expected production was as yet committed to paper.

In the opinion of Mr. Lovaine Mr. Benson was actually raised by this change of conduct, not only because he considered such devotion to his profession as praiseworthy in: the extreme, but because he was much impressed with the good taste and tact which he displayed in not continuing to offer him his advice, when the object for which it had originally been asked was happily completed. When, however, his powerful influence no longer served as a counteracting and superior force to the letters of Mrs. Lovaine, they did not fail to have considerable effect both upon Mr. Lovaine and his nephew.

Herbert began by alluding to the injustice of the expressions used by his aunt towards him upon the subject of Lord Goldsborough. ⸲ Mr. Lovaine, on the other hand, thought fit to uphold the dicta of his wife, not merely because she was his wife, but because he happened, in the present instance, to be of the same opinion as herself. The language which she adopted in her correspondence with respect to Herbert, naturally tended to foment any little irritation produced by such discussion, and consequently slight disagreements again took place; and though from the circumstance of no positive cause of absolute quarrel occurring, they continued on apparently good terms, the regrets which were expressed by Mr. Lovaine, that Herbert was again so altered for the worse, and by Herbert that it was so impossible to alter his uncle permanently for the better, made it very obvious that their feelings towards each other were not such as to preclude the possibility, should the occasion offer, of another rupture, similar to that which had been so judiciously made up by Mr. Benson.

CHAPTER XI.

THE time for the return of Mrs. Lovaine and her daughter to England was almost fixed, and Mr. Lovaine had determined to wait their arrival in London; for as Elinor's fortune was now considered to be made, her mother had consented to spend but a short time in the metropolis previous to their settling at Beechwood Park, where they intend to remain till Lord Goldsborough's presence would render their removal back to London indispensable, for the purpose of settlements, completion of *trousseau,* the purchase of jewels, and all such

necessary preliminaries to young ladies changing their name and condition, and without
which a marriage, in the opinion of Mrs.
Lovaine, would scarcely be valid.

Poor Mr. Lovaine was, however, doomed
to endure the delay of that happiness which
he so fondly hoped to derive from the complete
reunion of his family. Elinor was, as we mentioned once before, of too delicate a frame to
bear with impunity any very great stress,
either on her mind or body. She suffered at
Venice from the effects of over bodily fatigue;
and she was fated at Rheims to feel the bad
effects of over agitation, produced by the events
of the latter part of their *séjour* at Spa.

At Venice an accidental cold had, from a
previous state of excitement, assumed the form

of an alarming fever.   At Rheims a chill, occasioned by the rising of the fog from some low damp ground over which they had passed after sunset, occasioned a degree of illness, which alarmed Mrs. Lovaine so much, that fearful of finding themselves in a dirty French town, and still more dirty inn, without knowing to whom to apply for medical advice, she determined to reach Paris as soon as possible, thinking the journey.would probably prove a minor evil, (should her child fulfil the promise given of further illness, by its usual forerunner of racking head-ach, burning forehead, aching limbs, and parching thirst,) to that of the mismanagement of an obscure and ignorant doctor.

The day of their journey was one of great

anxiety to Mrs Lovaine, who trembled at every mile, lest she should not have adopted the wisest measure in proceeding on their journey, in spite of Elinor's alarming symptons: but she had afterwards good reason to rejoice at her decision, when experiencing all the kindness, attention, and skill of an English physician, resident with some acquaintance of her own, who, not venturing to trust their health to the management of the French faculty, had provided themselves with this luxury; not to say this *necessary* to the preservation of life on the Continent.

We do not mean to doubt the capability of French and Italian doctors to perform as many cures on their fellow-countrymen as are performed in England; but certain it is that no inflammation will tamely submit to resign its possession of English lungs, or fever of an English frame, when simply attacked by *tisanne;* and that such is the only weapon with which those maladies are sometimes attacked we can, if not from personal experience, yet from personal knowledge, vouch for as a fact.

Mrs. Lovaine had determined upon returning from Spa to England *vid* Paris, on pretence of choosing wedding clothes, and with the promise of its protracting but a very short time the period of their finally settling at home. But the fulfilment of this condition was no longer in her power. Elinor's illness proved to be a severe attack of ague, succeeded by a nervous fever. She was not considered to be in any positive danger, but her removal for a long, or indeed any definite time, became so entirely out of the question, that after frequent expressions of the wishes of Mrs. Lovaine, and of Elinor, that Mr. Lovaine should join them at Paris, and afterwards accompany them home; and being himself wearied with hope so long deferred, he sufficiently overcame his prejudices against quitting his native soil for a foreign land, actually to set sail for Calais; and in as short a time as particularly bad post-horses and a very uneasy carriage would take him, he arrived, to the unfeigned satisfaction of all three, at the residence of his wife and daughter at Paris.

Mr. Lovaine was perfectly horrified at finding his lady dressed *au dernier goût de Paris ;*

and would have been equally shocked at Elinor, had not her indisposition, and consequent *déshabille*, spared his eyes, at first, from seeing that they were both, what he called, " so confoundedly Frenchified."

Elinor was pale, and much reduced by her illness; but it was with no small pride that, notwithstanding these disadvantages, Mr. Lovaine discovered how much his darling girl had gained in personal appearance since they had parted; a circumstance which could not fail to give him pleasure; and the more so, as it was entirely unexpected: for Mrs. Lovaine, from whose sight she had rarely been absent an hour during their travels on the Continent, had scarcely herself been aware of the change which had taken place, and had very natu-

rally been silent on the subject. Mr. Lovaine's
pleasure, therefore, in finding that the half-
formed stripling looking girl of sixteen, was
transformed to his eyes, as it were at once,
from childhood into womanhood, was enhanced
by surprise; and it almost compensated to him
for the annoyance occasioned by the too frequent introduction of French or Italian words,
in the discourse of herself as well as her
mother: a habit which he highly deprecated,
but which, to a certain degree, is, without any
affectation, invariably acquired by a long residence abroad.

But whilst we leave Mr. Lovaine to the happiness of admiring his daughter, and to the
fascinations of the French capital, to overcome
in some degree his contempt and dislike to all

that did not exclusively belong to England, we must take the liberty of again crossing the water, to inform our readers of a transaction which took place between Herbert and his uncle, as it was one of very considerable importance to the prospects of our hero, previous to the departure of the latter for Paris.

Beechwood Park was in the immediate neighbourhood of a borough town, which having always been considered as a close borough, whose duty it was to obey the commands of its owner, or patron, Sir Thomas Danby, and thereby to return himself and another member of his nomination to Parliament, as the proper representatives of the free and independent burgesses of the town, Mr. Lovaine had never thought fit to interfere in its elective franchise, even in those times when his age and habits would have been less incompatible with a Parliamentary, and consequently a London life, than they had since become.

This long-established arrangement was, however, very unexpectedly deranged by the sudden death of Sir Thomas Danby himself. To his property his infant daughter was sole heiress; and although she had attained the power of very distinctly articulating the only two words spoken by a large portion of the great national assembly, "aye," and "no," yet her age and sex formed two insuperable bars to the possibility of her succeeding her father as Member of the lower House.

Mr. Lovaine was well known to be "rich in land and store;" therefore, with that disinterested feeling, and that independent generosity, which so eminently distinguishes the freeholders of a borough town in general, and of a close borough in particular, the electors determined upon offering the vacant seat to be at the disposal of the owner of Beechwood Park; and a deputation was accordingly sent to assure Mr. Lovaine of their readiness to abide by his superior wisdom in the choice of their future representative.

The message was received, and the proposal accepted, like most other messages or proposals of a flattering or agreeable import, very graciously, for although, as we have said before, Mr. Lovaine had no thoughts himself of recommencing a Parliamentary life, yet he was far from insensible to the increase of conse-

quence thus acquired, by the power of returning a Member to Parliament. Little as he had
hitherto been pleased at the turn for studious
occupation evinced by Herbert, it did occur to
him upon the present occasion, that it might
prove of some service to him, now that so fair
an opportunity for the display of his natural
and acquired powers offered itself in the prospect of a seat in Parliament; and he felt more
disposed to forgive that change in his character
and pursuits which had so long vexed and annoyed him, than he had ever done before.
" Besides," said he to himself, " when the
foolish boy is once in the House of Com-
mons, he will find himself obliged to leave off
talking some of that d—d radical stuff which
he acquired when he was in love with Mrs.

Lawlie; nothing puts such an effectual stop
to the eloquence of a clamorous advocate for
Parliamentary Reform, as benefiting himself
by the easily purchased votes of a highly venal borough;" (and in this opinion we cannot
but think that Mr. Lovaine was not very much
mistaken.) " If all the champions of the people, all the lovers of civil liberty, the friends
of universal suffrage, could but just be the
chosen representative of the smallest borough
in Cornwall; be destined to watch over the interests of from five to five and twenty burgesses,
who in spite of their oath to receive no benefit, prospectively or retrospectively, for their
support, have a fair and fixed price for their
vote, they would talk much less of the absolute necessity for those sinks of discontent

and disaffection, Birmingham and Manchester, being represented; and they would have a much better chance of being useful members of the community, than when they are endeavouring to disturb that order of things which has hitherto subsisted, and which has made us the first nation in the civilized world."

The idea that Herbert would ever dream of publicly declaring, or of acting upon the principles which he had with so much displeasure heard him advance in private, never occurred to him as possible. He looked too much upon political creeds as heir-looms, to think for a moment that his nephew could place himself under any other banners than those under which he had himself fought, and he would have presented him without scruple to the loyal borough of ———— as the highest of Tories, without even thinking it necessary to make any previous inquiries respecting his opinions on any great party question.

The sincerity of Herbert, however, spared his uncle the mortification of bringing in a man for the express purpose of opposing all those measures which he would have most warmly approved out of doors, and would, had he been in Parliament, have supported with equal warmth in-doors.

When sent by his uncle to learn the important communication that had been made to him of the kind disposition of the neighbouring freeholders to Beechwood Park, and of the equally kind intention of Mr. Lovaine to avail himself of the same for the purpose of giving his nephew an opportunity of distinguishing himself in public life, Herbert's first question was, "By what influence, Sir, would my election be secured?"

Mr. Lovaine assured him it would be by the usual influence of money, and such other favours as are never considered by either candidates or constituents to come under the head of bribery; and kindly added that he intended to charge himself with that part of the business.

Herbert coldly thanked him and looked grave, and appeared to be doubtful as to the propriety of accepting the offer.

Mr. Lovaine, surprised at this apparent indifference, or want of gratitude for his kind-

ness, asked him what the devil he was thinking
of, and whether, after all his repeated professions of patriotism, he was indisposed to profit
by the opportunity now offered of making
himself useful, or at least of learning how to do
so when he was wiser and older.

Herbert declared that his wish to be useful
to his country was quite as strong as ever.

" Well, then," replied Mr. Lovaine, ." you
had better set off for Beechwood Park the beginning of next week—to be present at your
election—to make speeches at the election dinner, and to dance with the girls at the election
ball; for, as our influence in the Borough is
newly acquired, it will be well for you to make
yourself popular: indeed, I feel half disposed

to accompany you myself, for I do not so much dislike the sort of thing as some people do; there is always much good fellowship at those kind of meetings. It will be but little trouble, for there seems to be no occasion to canvass the good people for their votes; indeed, Sir Thomas Danby and his friend were, I believe, very seldom present at their election."

Mr. Lovaine was quite right in supposing that the offer of a seat in Parliament would be agreeable to Herbert; but as he had no idea that he could entertain any scruples of availing himself of the usual means to that end, he was quite at a loss to understand his apparent hesitation and indecision; and was far from being pleased at his requesting to be allowed a few hours' deliberation, before he decided on accepting that which Mr. Lovaine thought would make him the happiest of mortals.

A few hours brought to Mr. Lovaine a note from his nephew, containing an acceptance, but a conditional acceptance, of the offer. He had sought Mr. Benson, to ask his advice on a matter on which, of all others, he was most desirous of obtaining it; for he and his followers had, in fact, from the first hour of their acquaintance, been his political preceptors. Mr. Benson could not be found; but in returning from the pursuit of him, he met their common friends, Messrs. Claypole and Ratsbane, and to them he imparted the dilemma in which his uncle's offer had placed him; and by their advice, and in concurrence with his own opinion, he determined upon so far sacrificing his principles, as to endure a minor evil for a major good : to accept the proffered seat, though unconstitutionally obtained, for the purpose of lifting up his voice on high against all that he disapproved, where that voice would be listened to, and supported, as it ever would be, by his most conscientious vote. The condition, therefore, on which, he informed his uncle, depended his acceptance, was, that of perfect independence as to the party which he might think fit to join, or the side which he might think proper to support of whatever question was brought forward.

Mr. Lovaine was indignant at the receipt of this note, and was at first determined to give up at once all idea of bringing forward a young man, so little qualified to fill the situation in which he had wished to place him. He had even nearly finished writing a few lines to him in reply, telling him that such was his determination, when the recollection of Herbert being the only male relation he possessed in the world—the only one that bore his name—his natural heir—the future possessor of Beechwood Park—therefore the person most interested in creating and preserving an interest in this particular Borough, made him pause, and finally relent, ere he concluded his letter. Herbert's conditional acceptance was reconsidered. The wish not to be fettered in his political career by the opinions of his uncle, appeared to have dictated the tone of independence in which the note had been

couched.   Nothing could be more improper,
not to say undutiful and impertinent, according to the estimate of Mr. Lovaine, both of
the value of his own judgment and experience,
and of the respect due from a son to a father
(for in that relation he generally considered
himself and his nephew to stand).   Still, as he
was anxious to bring him forward for the reasons above mentioned, his fault was sooner
pardoned than it would have been under any
other circumstances; and he charitably attributed the whole more to a boyish, not to say
childish, desire to act for himself, than to any
intention of acting in opposition to the principles in which he had been originally educated.

But although Mr. Lovaine was sufficiently

disposed to overlook the offence of Herbert's conditional acceptance, not at once to abandon the idea of bringing him into Parliament; yet, at the same time, he felt it would be necessary to ascertain whether he did or did not enter-tain political opinions at variance with his own. He scarcely expected to find, when Herbert was required to state positively what were his views and intentions, that they would differ in reality from his own; but he very wisely thought, that, since his nephew had made such a point of being considered a free and independent member, it would be well to possess their written declaration before he gave him the opportunity of acting up to them.

Destroying, therefore, the commencement of the reply which he had first intended to make to Herbert's note, Mr. Lovaine wrote and despatched another, requiring, ere he agreed to the proposed conditions of perfect freedom and independence, a written *exposé* of his whole political creed.

If Mr. Lovaine was offended at the stipulation made by his nephew, previous to his acceptance of what he considered, and very justly considered in some respects, an act of kindness, certain it was that Herbert was no less so at the manner in which he was desired to declare, not so much his sentiments, as his intentions of voting upon all those questions, the support or opposition of which generally determines the party to which a Member is considered to belong. Herbert would not have thought it necessary to consult with his

friends, as to the proper method of replying to
his uncle's requisition, because an unhesitating
avowal of the truth would at all times have
appeared to him the proper course to pursue;
but Mr. Claypole, one of the gentlemen whose
advice he had asked as to the propriety of
accepting, under any circumstances, the proffered seat for a close borough, happening to
be at dinner with him when the letter from
his uncle arrived, he imparted to him both its
contents, and his own determination to be perfectly open and explicit in his reply.

CHAPTER XII.

Mr. Claypole was a red-hot, uncompro-
mising radical; a reformer of every thing,
whether right or wrong. He had with much
greater vehemence, and with full as much sincerity as Herbert, adopted all the opinions, and,
if we may venture so to express it, the slang,
both in thought and expression, that Mr. Benson, Mrs. Lawlie, and others of the same party
had taught him. He was not, unfortunately,
without sufficient quickness to deceive both
himself and others as to the extent of his
abilities, wholly without that sobriety of judg-

ment which enables a man to consider calmly both sides of the question, ere he comes to his own conclusion, and equally unblessed with those rare and beautiful qualities, candour and modesty, which teach a man alike to listen with attention and toleration to the opinions and prejudices of others, and to mistrust the infallibility of his own. He was perfectly incapable of directing with wisdom or discretion the conduct of himself, and still less that of any friend; and when he had rushed headlong into the very thick of an argument which he could not reasonably support, and in which he was defeated, he invariably became so irascible, that his life had more than once been placed in some jeopardy from the warmth with which he had defended the cause he had thus espoused

with more zeal than ability. Still, inconsistent
as it may appear, with such glaring defects,
Mr. Claypole was not without some power of
influencing those with whom he associated.
Fluent in speech, earnest in feeling, and positive in opinion, he sometimes persuaded where
he could not convince; and with that quickness, to which he was principally indebted for
his reputation for talent, he seldom failed to
find some plausible excuse for the miscarriage
of his purpose, that should in no way impugn
the wisdom and justice of his judgment or
advice.

It certainly was not to be expected that
Herbert should receive from such a counsellor
as Mr. Claypole, much encouragement to
frame the political creed which his uncle had
somewhat imperatively called for, in the terms

best calculated to reconcile Mr. Lovaine to those differences of opinion, which he considered himself now obliged to avow as existing between them, upon most subjects connected with the legislation of their country.

Herbert was urged by his companion not only to give expression to every sentiment that must infallibly prove a subject of discord between him and his parliamentary patron, but even to outstep his feelings in their expression.

" If," said Mr. Claypole, " your uncle wishes in any one instance to influence your vote, *i. e.* if he considers the entertaining of certain opinions at variance with his own, an objection to his giving you the means of coming into Parliament, it clearly proves that it is not his intention to bring you in as a free and independent member; and to accept a seat, without at least that compensation for the otherwise almost insuperable evil of representing the venal burgesses of a small close borough, (who barter their honourable privileges for the filthy lucre of gain) would be indeed unworthy of those principles to which, I trust and believe, you are a true and sincere friend. Do not throw away this opportunity of shewing that a lover of liberty scorns to truckle for a little brief authority. Do not let it be in the power of any man living to say that for the gratification of your wishes you were ready to abandon your principles. If you do not declare your determination to advocate every opinion most contrary to those entertained by

your uncle, you may subject yourself hereafter
to the imputation of inconsistent, perhaps of
dishonourable conduct towards him; he will
naturally endeavour to fetter you in every
way. Do not therefore hesitate to shew him
at once how widely it is possible to differ from
him. Should you, as I trust you will not, be
induced, when in Parliament, to coincide with
that party held most in reverence by Mr. Lovaine, he will naturally rejoice at the circumstance; and you will meet with no reproaches
for having deviated from the path in which he
was led to expect you would tread. But, on
the other hand, if you at this moment acknowledge your agreement with him upon any
one subject, and have, as you probably will
have, reason to change that opinion upon fur-

ther consideration, this written declaration which you are now called upon to make, will be quoted upon you. You may be accused of deceit, of currying favour at the expense of truth; you may perhaps be threatened, nay even actually required to give up your seat, on the plea of your having obtained it on false pretences."

Such arguments were not likely to fall in vain on the ears of Herbert; they were too well calculated to arouse a spirit like his, not materially to affect both the manner and the matter of his reply to his uncle. He was even occasionally assisted by Mr. Claypole in its composition, and the whole was inspected and approved by him before it was despatched to its final destination.

The perusal of this letter was a severe blow
to poor Mr. Lovaine; he read, and re-read
with pain and indignation the melancholy confirmation of his worst, though hitherto slightest
fears. He had had occasionally, from the moment of Herbert's first hesitation in accepting
the proffered honour of representing the borough
of ———, what is commonly called qualms
respecting his principles; but he had always
rejected the dreadful suspicion of his intending
the first opportunity to publicly support and
advance, what he had ever flattered himself
was but the idle talk of a young man, pleased,
though misled, by the first-fruits of knowledge,
as he would have done the disagreeable impression of a painful dream. He could not
believe in the possibility of a youth, educated

as Herbert had been, under his own immediate auspices, being so changed: his vexation was not therefore unmixed with surprise.

Mr. Lovaine forgot, alas! like many others who have had the heavy responsibility of education upon their shoulders, that although he had sent his ward to school and college, because it was an established custom there to send boys, he had never, in fact, at any time, taken any trouble to ascertain what he there acquired—what degree of improvement he made—or what progress in learning he attained.

Though few people might have been disposed to exert their borough interest in favour of one directly opposed to them upon every subject, yet many would have regarded that

contrariety of opinion, with toleration, and
simply as an obstacle to their rendering them
any assistance in their parliamentary election.
But to Mr. Lovaine such a difference of opinion as was expressed in the political declaration set forth by Herbert, could not be looked
upon with the composure with which even he
would, perhaps, have viewed what might be
considered the errors of judgment. He regarded it as an entire loss of character; and
enraged beyond description, not only at the
want of deference for the principles to which
he (Mr. Lovaine) had been always attached,
but at the total want of respect to himself,
which was too clearly shewn in the joint composition of Herbert and Mr. Claypole, he
paced up and down the room in a state of

considerable agitation, endeavouring to determine what line of conduct it would be best
to pursue.

All idea of giving Herbert the means of
publicly disgracing himself and his family was,
of course, at once rejected. The recollection
of their former, though recent quarrel, came to
his mind; he reproached himself with having
too easily given in upon that occasion, and to
that circumstance attributed the presumption
now shewn by his nephew in thus insulting
him. Every trifling disagreement—every trivial dispute that had ever occurred between
them for ages past, now came before his eyes,
and were seen as through a magnifying glass;
every thing seemed to rise in importance in
his sight that could tend to irritate him against

Herbert; his only feeling of self-reproach being that of over-indulgence, and thinking he
had lowered his dignity, by overlooking too
easily the various offences committed against
the authority, to which his years, his relationship, and his position entitled him. He determined to take this opportunity of teaching
his nephew that he would no longer patiently
submit to such conduct, and that he should
learn to rue the day when he had first flattered himself that either the adoption, or the
avowal of the principles and opinions contained in his epistle should pass unpunished.

With this determination Mr. Lovaine composed himself sufficiently to address a few lines
to Herbert; reproaching him bitterly for his
ungrateful and undutiful disposition, refusing

not only to take any further steps in the
matter that had called forth this correspondence, but even to admit him into his presence; declining indeed all future intercourse
with him, until time or repentance should have
wrought such a change in his character and
principles, as would render the repetition of
similar conduct perfectly impossible.

It was but a short time after the despatch
of this letter, before the solitude of Mr. Lovaine was interrupted by an accidental visit
from Mr. Benson. The state of agitation into
which something had thrown the former, could
not escape the quick observation of the latter;
and although he abstained from any direct
interrogatory, Mr. Lovaine felt that it would
be in vain to attempt concealing the want of

composure from his penetrating glance. Perhaps he would, at any rate, have been glad to unburthen his bosom to one, for whose character and sense he entertained so high an opinion; or possibly he was encouraged by perceiving that his countenance and manner were readily understood by his companion; but certain it is, that in a very short time Mr. Benson was made entire master of every detail of the quarrel that had taken place between the Messrs. Lovaine, senior and junior.

Mr. Benson was, as usual, all attention to whatever was communicated to him by Mr. Lovaine. He expressed his deep regret that Herbert should have given him so much cause of uneasiness; he heard himself, with some complacency, reproached for having so misplaced his kindness, as to have assisted in reconciling them after their first quarrel; he faintly offered a repetition of the same good offices: which having been warmly and positively rejected, though not without a few passing compliments for his excess of good-nature to such an unworthy friend, he next mildly inquired what steps he intended taking respecting the representation of the borough, which had been the innocent cause of so much trouble. But how to act upon this point was a dilemma which, in Mr. Lovaine's first burst of indignation against his nephew, had been entirely overlooked.

" To lose so valuable a possession, Sir, as the power of returning a member to parliament, might perhaps, prove hereafter a subject of regret to you," said Mr. Benson, " and yet, unless you avail yourself of the offer when made, it may be difficult to regain that power. It is generally easier to *retain* than to *obtain.*"

" True," replied Mr. Lovaine, " but, my dear Benson, I am too old now to begin a new course of life; a man, when he professes to serve his country in any way, should be actively employed in the fulfilment of his duty, and it would not suit me to alter all my habits. Herbert is my only near male relation. I have hitherto treated him as a son and heir; though unless a most complete reform takes place in his whole character before my death, I could scarcely answer it to my conscience to leave my property in the guardianship of such hands. My cousins, who are next in degrees of relationship, are still minors. I really know not what to do "

" Perhaps, Sir, some friend or connexion, on whose honour you might perfectly depend, would undertake to perform the part of what is called a stop-gap. Herbert will not, I feel confident, long merit your displeasure, and you would then regret having it no longer in your power to bring him forward into public life."

" I am less sanguine of his' reformation, Benson, than you would kindly pursuade me to be," replied Mr. Lovaine.

A dead silence ensued. It was not the business of Mr. Benson unnecessarily to contradict, and Mr. Lovaine appeared for some few minutes to be wholly engrossed by his own thoughts. At last, looking up at his visitor with that air of satisfaction which generally shews that the labour of thought has been rewarded by the birth of a new idea, he asked him whether it would be agreeable to him to perform that part himself which he had so very amicably recommended for the sake of Herbert, and consent to be the representative of the borough of ———, till such time as, from any change in the principles of his nephew, or the coming of age of his eldest cousin, he should desire the election of one of his own family.

Mr. Benson at first appeared disposed to hesitate. He feared that, unless Mr. Lovaine would consent to his giving a full explanation

to Herbert of the terms on which he had accepted such kindness, his motives might be
misconstrued, and that he might become liable
to the unjust suspicion of having usurped the
rights of his friend. To this proposition Mr.
Lovaine entirely declined acceding, because he
wished that no hope of forgiveness should be
held out to his nephew at that moment; and
he then so clearly pointed out to Mr. Benson
the folly of being influenced by the fear of an
unjust suspicion, as well as the gratitude which
Herbert would one day feel towards him,
should he ever become worthy of the friendship
of such a true friend as himself, that his
scruples were at last overcome, and he accepted, with a degree of thankfulness well
pleasing to a man of Mr. Lovaine's character,

the offer of adding the weight of his wisdom to that of the great National Assembly.

We must, in justice to the consistency of Mr. Benson's character, suppose that it was not without a severe struggle with his former and openly avowed principles, that he accepted the offer made to him by a High Tory, of representing a close borough. As, however, he was more successful than Herbert had been in overcoming these scruples, and gave no utterance to them, we cannot be considered bound to pry into his thoughts, or to give publicity to that which (judging by his silence) he wished to keep private.

Delighted with his new arrangement, Mr. Lovaine agreed to accompany Mr. Benson the following morning to Beechwood Park, where they were to remain a day or two previous to that of the election, for the purpose of making themselves popular with those who were equally determined conscientiously to vote according to the price agreed on for their so doing, whether they ever beheld their members or not.　　　ᴉ

That Mr. Lovaine should not discover, during their political discussions, (which naturally arose from the object of their journey,) the existence of any very particular difference between the opinions of himself and his *protégé*, was, it must be confessed, rather to the credit of Mr. Benson's ingenuity, than to the discredit of Mr. Lovaine's powers of discernment; for how could he imagine that when Mr. Benson perfectly agreed with him as to the expediency of certain measures for the

preservation of the dignity of the aristocracy,
he was, in fact, only agreeing with him as to
the expediency of the means, while he was
secretly denying the desirableness of the end;
that he was all the time heartily wishing that
the whole body could be suddenly obligéd to
eat their bread by the sweat of their brow;
and that he himself could stand in their shoes.
How could he possibly divine that, when he
praised what he was pleased to call that mystic
union of Church and State, as one of the
strong bulwarks to our happy form of government, and that Mr. Benson assented to its
power, that he was silently dissenting from his
application of the word " happy," even to the
degree of considering a republic highly prefer-
able to a monarchy.   How, in short, could Mr.

Lovaine be expected to discover, that when, upon these and many other subjects, Mr. Benson appeared so perfectly to agree with him in the deductions drawn from a certain hypothesis, that it was only the deduction to which he agreed, and that he in his heart denied, and had, elsewhere, often and openly denied, the truth of the hypothesis.

Perhaps, when once secure of what he could not but consider as the utmost good ever likely to arise from the patronage of Mr. Lovaine, Mr. Benson might have become less reserved as to his general view of men and things: but Mr. Lovaine was spared for the time the mortification of discovering how completely his penetration could be blinded, and his judgment warped by prejudice; for almost immediately after the election, and his return to town from Beechwood Park, he quitted London for Paris, to join, as we have already stated, his wife and invalid daughter.

CHAPTER XIII.

THE first intimation which Herbert received
of the election of Mr. Benson was from its
announcement in the newspapers. Mr. Benson had left London the morning following
that on which Herbert had received the prohi-
bition from Mr. Lovaine to appear again in
his presence; he could of course, therefore,
know nothing verbally of the arrangement
from him, and it could hardly be expected
that, at such a moment, the incipient Member
should have found time for such an unpleasant
and difficult task as writing to his *ci-devant*

friend a full explanation of how the abandon-
ment of popular principles had taken place
from pure patriotism, and shewing that the
supplanting his friend was a genuine act of
friendship.

Herbert could scarcely believe his eyes when
he read the paragraph which proclaimed these
two circumstances, by notifying the election of
Mr. Benson. He instantly sought his fellow-
pupil, Mr. Claypole, to know whether he had
been informed of this deviation in their preceptor from his precepts; but found that his
knowledge of the event had only been obtained from the newspapers. Mr. Benson had
considerable influence over the mind of Mr.
Claypole, whenever he took the pains to exercise it, but not having done so, as yet, on the

present occasion, he gave vent to the natural impetuosity of his feelings, and greatly assisted in fanning the flame of wrath that was already kindled in the bosom of Herbert against his former ally.

The result of this interview and cogitation was a letter addressed to Mr. Benson from Herbert, reminding him of all his former professions respecting the freedom of election, and taxing him, in a most unequivocal manner, with one of the most flagrant acts of political tergiversation of which a man could be guilty. (Perhaps, and not unnaturally, he was the more provoked at this conduct in his Mentor, as had he felt sure of his adopting or sanctioning such a line, he would himself have felt somewhat less scruple in accepting more graciously, and less conditionally, the offer made to him by his uncle). He reproached him with having fomented the quarrel which had taken place between his uncle and himself, for the advancement of his own views; and, in short, he called him to account for his thoughts, words, and deeds, in such a manner, that Mr. Benson, being somewhat perplexed to know how to reply to accusations so difficult to answer, and not being deficient in personal courage, considered his *honour* insulted, and lost no time in demanding the particular satisfaction of being shot at, or shooting the man whom he had injured. It certainly was an illogical and an unphilosophic mode of settling the affair.; but as it presented, upon the whole, the fewest difficulties to the mind of Mr. Benson, he sent for Claypole, as a common friend, to be the bearer of his answer to Herbert. He did not, however, fail, during Mr. Claypole's visit, to exercise his wonted influence over him, and entirely to change the opinion he had at first entertained respecting his recent conduct, and which had, in fact, so greatly contributed to strengthen that of Herbert, as to have induced him to write the offensive letter in question.

Mr. Claypole was far from wishing that matters should proceed to these extremities. He had no desire whatever to undertake the disagreeable office of second in a duel, or to run the risk of losing, by death or banishment, one or both of such friends as Messrs. Benson and Lovaine—revering, as he did, the

talents of the one, and (as we trust these pages
may never come before his eyes, we will venture to, say,) the birth and. situation of the
other.٭ He was, therefore, the best person that
could have been selected to avert the im-
pending. evil; and it must be acknowledged
that he shewed as much skill, and more good˙
sense, in preventing the fatal consequences that
might have ensued from the correspondence
between his friends, than that which he had
displayed in exciting Herbert to commence it.

. He turned every little concession that was
made by either party to. the greatest possible
advantage; in short, he rested not till he had
succeeded in satisfying the honour of both,
without the further risk of bloodshed.

-Herbert and Mr. Benson were reconciled;

but not restored to their former friendship and
intimacy. Herbert feeling that he had been
intemperate, perhaps even unjust, in some
of the expressions relating to the conduct
of Mr. Benson towards himself, of which he
had made use in his letter, had been less back-
ward in listening to the overtures of peace
which were offered by Mr. Claypole than he
might otherwise have been; but although he
was persuaded that he had less to resent personally concerning the seat in Parliament than
he at first imagined, yet he could not disguise
from himself that Mr. Benson had abandoned
the principles to which he had pretended the
greatest attachment. He had thought him a
patriot, and found him a mercenary; he had
believed him capable of acting up to his pro-

fessions at any sacrifice, and had discovered him willing to abandon them for the temporary gratification of his vanity and ambition. The delusion was over, as though a film had fallen from his eyes. He still admired Mr. Benson's talents, but he no longer viewed his character and conduct through the medium of that halo of brightness, with which his own ardent imagination had surrounded them. Many little circumstances, too trifling and unimportant to be worth recording, relating to Mr. Benson's intimacy with Mr. Lovaine, and which, at the time, he had willingly attributed to accident, or to misunderstanding on his own part, now struck him in a different light, and greatly tended to increase his suspicions of the consistency of Mr. Benson's conduct, and of the sincerity of his character.

It is always mortifying and distressing to be compelled to think less well of a friend than we have hitherto done; there is so much pleasure in admiring what we love—in the belief that perfection exists where we have placed our esteem or affection—that it cannot be foregone without pain. To mistrust the justice of our admiration is one of the hardest lessons taught by experience; yet it must be learned, like many other things that we should be happier could we never know.

Herbert was far from being easy or comfortable under the circumstances of the complete rupture that had taken place between his uncle and himself; and the less so, as his confidence in those upon whose principles he thought he had acted, was now somewhat diminished. He had discovered that Mr. Claypole was a man who was swayed by the passion of the moment; and while regretting that he had been so much guided by his advice, in the letters which he had addressed both to his uncle and to Mr. Benson, he, not unnaturally, felt less disposed than formerly, to seek his society or respect his opinion.

To hear nothing from or of Elinor, who was not permitted by Mrs. Lovaine to write to her cousin on account of the Goldsborough heresy, or by Mr. Lovaine on account of the quarrel, was also a source of much annoyance to him. He felt, in short, for the first time in his life, that worst of solitudes,- *viz.* being alone in a multitude. He had dropped or offended so many of his old friends and acquaintance, that they naturally sought him no more; and though he would on no account have owned, even to himself, that he regretted that society which he had quitted voluntarily, we have but very little doubt that the feeling of being neglected tended greatly, however insensibly, to increase the depression of spirits under which, at this period, he began frequently to labour.

He employed much of his time (which was now almost uninterruptedly at his own disposal) in the cultivation of his mind. Often in a fit of low spirits did he imagine that his ambition was deadened, and his prospects blighted.

Still he neglected not his studies—the pursuit
of real knowledge had taken place of the love
of display—the more he learnt, the more he
condemned the hastiness with which he had
formed his opinions upon those subjects which
most demanded deliberation and research, and
the more did he daily feel the wisdom of that
Poet who has said, that

" A little learning is a dangerous thing."

Nor was it possible for the truth of these reflections to strike thus home to his mind,
without its also suggesting some regrets at the
recollection of his late intolerance towards
each and every one who had presumed to differ from him, and from those whom he reve-
renced and followed in habits or opinions—
and it would have been as amusing to an unin-

terested observer of human nature, as pleasing
to the real well-wisher of young Lovaine, to
have seen the difference of reception with
which the hearty cordial greeting of Lord
Blaney Mount Shannon (who was accidentally in London for a few days) was met, to
that which was bestowed on the ill-timed, 'but
well-intended civility of poor Sir Gilbert
Bayley, when he had the bad luck innocently
to interrupt an interesting discussion between
Herbert and Mr. Benson.

A few days subsequent to the rencontre of
Herbert with Lord Blaney, he set out from
his lodgings, in order to perform his promise
of calling upon Lady Blaney. The day and
the hour had been of his own appointment, and
he therefore felt bound to keep the engage-

ment, though not being very well, (for the sedentary life he now led often affected his health) and feeling unusually depressed in spirits, he was not particularly inclined to listen to Lady Blaney's report of what Mr. Cartwright had said of Johnny's teeth, or of what Mr. Brodie had thought best for poor little Pussy's spine. Perhaps, indeed, it would have been better, had he not scrupulously kept his engagement, for he conferred almost as little pleasure as he received by fulfilling it.

" What can have happened to Mr. Lovaine, my dear?" said Lady Blaney to her husband, ere Herbert had quite closed the door; " he is become either the most absent or the most unfeeling man alive. I cannot conceive what could make you think him so much altered for the better."

" He certainly struck me, when I met him the other day, as being much more pleasing and agreeable than when we last saw him at Beechwood Park. But how has he offended you ?"

" Offended! oh no ! I am not actually offended; but I must say, I think him very disagreeable : he took no more notice of the dear children than if they had not been in the room; and when I told him what a little hero Johnny had been in having his tooth out, he said, " I am very sorry—I hope he will be a better boy another time ;" and when I told him how much it had cost us to leave our other four little treasures in the country, he merely remarked, " What a comfort !" In short, during his whole visit, he scarcely seemed to know where he was, or what he was about : if it had been in the evening, I should have known to what to attribute it; but as it was in the morning, I can only suppose it was *finery*."

Lord Blaney took his young friend's part as well as he could : but quite in vain, for nothing could be more just than the accusation of in-attention brought against her visitor by Lady Blaney; though she did him injustice in ascribing the cause to what she termed *sheer finery.* He had certainly been most painfully *distrait* during the whole time of his visit; but the cause of this unwonted state of abstraction will, perhaps, be better understood, when we relate a little occurrence that took place on his way to the much-aggrieved Lady Blaney.

Herbert's attention had been arrested by the sight of some new prints in the window of a shop adjoining one of those fashionable

dépôts for every article necessary to female
attire. Several coachmen were there awaiting
the sound of that well-known call of their
lady's name, and the sight of that particular
man, who is kept at such shops, solely to
assist the footmen in handing customers and
parcels back to the carriage from whence they
came—to announce that the pattern was
matched, or the gown chosen, and that the
fair purchasers were ready to set out in pursuit
of more goods, to prove that they are not,
" when unadorned, adorned the most," or to
leave their card upon many a nominal friend,
who has as strictly forbid their admittance, as
they sincerely hope it will not be granted.
Herbert stood for some little time examining
the objects which had attracted his notice,
when the call for Mrs. Gordon's carriage, that

created instantly a responsive movement in a smart, active, well-powdered footman, fell upon his ear. He turned his head almost involuntarily, to see the lady who bore a name that had for some time past been one of deeper interest to him than he cared to allow.

The lady was occupied in watching the advance of the carriage from the further end of the street, and her head was averted; still Herbert felt almost sure that he could not be mistaken in the figure. He would have passed in front of her, in hope of seeing her face, but something seemed to rivet him to the spot, and he stirred not an inch. The door was opened —the lady had got her foot upon the first step: Herbert despaired of being able to ascertain whether he was mistaken in her identity, when a shopman ran out of the shop, apparently to ask for something;—the carriage pockets were searched, and a card was given. In giving the card she turned her face, and Herbert had a full view of her whom he had known as Emily De Clifford. She was accompanied by another lady, who had remained in the carriage: of her face he did not obtain a sight; but her general effect too much resembled that of Lady Harriet, for him to doubt that Emily's companion was any other than her mother.

As soon as the carriage had fairly driven off, Herbert was seized with an irresistible desire to purchase instantly a new pair of gloves, of that particular shopman to whom Emily had given her address. Moreover he had almost determined to inquire of him not only the price of the said gloves, but also the

name of his last customer.   He was, however,
spared the disagreeable necessity of asking
such information as the latter, for the card
which had just been received was laid upon
the counter while the gloves were sought for,
and Herbert instantly read the address, which
was no other than ' Mrs. Gordon, at Lord
Melrose's, Grosvenor Square.'   He could not,
however, resist asking the man, when he returned well laden with a handsome variety of
the article demanded, whether the lady who
had just left the shop was Mrs. Gordon.

   " Yes, Sir,—this pair will fit you exactly,
Sir—very lately married, I believe, Sir."

   This answer, so carelessly given, confirmed
his worst fears.   No gloves would fit—his hand
shook—he tore two pair to pieces in trying
them on, and walked out of the shop as much

offended with the shopman, who required to be paid for the torn pairs, as if they could have been useful to any body else.

When Herbert retired to bed that night, it must be owned that it was not to sleep. " I have lost her, and by my own fault !" was instantly the thought that haunted his mind and disturbed his peace. When an evil is but in anticipation, hope can still tell a flattering tale; its extent can only be known and truly felt when it is passed.

END OF VOL. II.

LONDON.
J. L. Cox, Printer, G eat Queen Street.